What Color are Your Assets?
An Insider's Guide to Rare Coins and Precious Metals

by

Lawrence D. Goldberg

What Color are Your Assets?
An Insider's Guide to Rare Coins and Precious Metals

by

Lawrence D. Goldberg

Cover design by Bryan Stoughton

ISBN-10: 1-933990-27-9
ISBN-13: 978-1-933990-27-9

Published by
Zyrus Press, Inc.
P.O. Box 17810
Irvine, CA 92623

Printed in the United States of America

About the Author

Lawrence D. Goldberg began his career in rare coins in 1981, working for Bowers and Ruddy Galleries in Hollywood, CA. After working as an independent consultant for several other companies, he founded Customized Numismatic Portfolios, Inc. in 1991. He has written and published his thrice-annual *Rare Coin Report Newsletter* since 2001. He is an authorized dealer for PCGS, NGC, CAC and is an associate member of PNG.

Outside of the rare coin industry, he wrote the debt management e-book *Balance Transfer Magic*, and spearheaded the successful effort to raise money to build a new outdoor stage for the Independent Shakespeare Co. of Los Angeles. In the 1980s he was an active member of the California Libertarian Party and a frequent guest editorialist on KNX news radio.

In addition to an active interest in political and economic issues, he follows advances in astronomy and space science, an area of fascination since childhood. He holds a bachelor's degree in literature with minors in drama and political science from Whitman College in Walla Walla, WA, where he graduated summa cum laude, Phi Beta Kappa. A native of San Francisco, he remains an avid Giant and 49er fan.

Acknowledgements

THROUGHOUT MY 32 YEARS IN RARE COINS, numerous dealers and numismatists have been extremely generous with their knowledge, expertise and advice. Chief among them are Wayne Wojdak and Steve Wojdak, who taught me the business and to whom I will be forever grateful. William Paul and Leonard Shafer, both recently deceased, whose generosity of spirit and willingness to share their vast resources of knowledge are irreplaceable. Others deserving particular thanks include Marc Crane, Doug Winter, Don Kagin, Dennis Gillio and Ron Karp.

I may have written the words, but without the superlative support of many people *What Color Are Your Assets?* would not be a book. Invaluable contributions through their feedback and suggestions were made by Wendy Taylor, John Cooper, Don Kagin, my daughter Ashley Bank, and most particularly my associate Mike Clarke, whose relentless tenacity and dedication to making this book the best it could be were extraordinary. Nor would this book be reality without the herculean effort and expertise of Zyrus Press editor Bruce Porter. I would also like to thank the readers of my *Rare Coin Report Newsletter* who provided continual feedback on that publication, and who asked the many questions which became the basis and the reason for writing this book. Special thanks to Bill Salameh who suggested the title.

I also am beholden to my brother, Steve, and sisters, Dena and Kayla, for their encouragement and emotional support, but most especially to my loving wife and life partner Philleen Meskin, who not only helped with the text, but provided amazing emotional support at a level that makes me feel like the luckiest man alive.

This book is dedicated to my parents, Tannette Estelle Goldberg (1926-2013) who — among so much more — taught me to never give up and Daniel T. Goldberg, who at age 98 continues to be a fountainhead of support and inspiration.

Lawrence D. Goldberg
Burbank, California
October 2013

Table of Contents

Foreword

BEING A RARE COIN DEALER IS FREQUENTLY like teaching a class with a revolving roster of students where the semester never ends. While each person and their needs are individual and different, many of the same questions and issues arise and must be addressed again and again. As one who does not like to repeat the same work over and over again, I took it upon myself to write a basic guide that would save time and enable my clients to get the answers they sought.

That is why the working title of this book was "Answers to the 20 Questions Most Frequently Asked of Rare Coin Dealers."

Additionally, I was motivated by hearing far too many horror stories of people who bought rare coins or precious metals without knowing basic information. This made them easy marks for high pressure salespeople who might feed them inaccurate information or unrealistic expectations, with the inevitable result that they needlessly overpaid, or bought inferior material, and lost tremendous amount of money in the process.

What started as a simple series of essays gradually grew into something much more comprehensive, and this book is the result. Regardless of the final form, my original purpose was to create a concise yet complete resource for investors and collectors.

Yes, it was a challenge, but delving into issues that after more than 30 years in the business I often took for granted has not only been very satisfying and a great deal of fun, but has given me a new outlook and a fresh vision. It is the ideal kind of unintended consequence.

It is my hope and intention that using this book will enhance your confidence, financial effectiveness and enjoyment of your involvement with rare coins and precious metals.

Introduction

THE ARENA OF HARD ASSETS, WHICH INCLUDES rare coins, gold, silver and other precious metals, has a long and storied history, dating back to before Biblical times, through the Greek and Roman classical era, the Middle Ages, the Renaissance, the Industrial Revolution and now the Information Age.

It is a story that continues today because in our complex society of worldwide computer-aided markets — trading everything from stocks and bonds to currencies, commodities and every other type of good or service — the subject of money remains as basic to our survival as food and shelter.

For many the subject brings up a wide variety of questions. The aim of this book is to explore the circumstances behind those questions and provide a common sense approach of how to successfully navigate the hard asset marketplace. Below is a sampling of the frequently asked questions this book addresses, information useful to the active collector and investor as well as the beginner:

- Why buy gold, silver or rare coins?
- How does the economy affect rare coins and precious metals?
- Are rare coins a good investment?
- Which coins will make the most money?
- What are the risks of owning hard assets?

- What are the best ways to work with a dealer?
- What do I do with my inherited coins?
- What are the best ways to buy and sell?
- Do I need to take physical possession?
- Is silver a better investment than gold?
- How do I avoid being ripped off, either by thieves or by dealers?
- What role do collectors play in all this?
- Will coins make me more money than stocks?
- How do I buy and sell without a dealer?
- Should I buy silver coins or silver bars?
- How do I know which hard assets are best for me?
- Should I get my coins professionally certified?
- Is the dollar going to collapse?
- What are *price spreads* and how are they used?
- How do I know if I'm buying and selling at fair prices?
- What is the long-term outlook?
- What should I know about storing coins safely?
- Where do I get good information about hard assets?

You will also learn how gold, silver and rare coins function as monetary instruments, what has sparked the recent dramatic bull market in the precious metals, and ultimately the basic framework from which to harness the hard asset market to your maximum benefit.

Overview

Gold, Silver and Rare Coins:
The Economics that Drive these Markets

GOLD, SILVER AND RARE COINS MAY BE the subject of this book, but in a very real sense it is all about money. At its core, money is a vehicle of trade and a storehouse of value. Gold, silver and rare coins are also vehicles of trade and storehouses of value. They don't do anything else. And yet, people have lost a great deal of money — and missed out on excellent value enhancing opportunities — because this simple fact was ignored, and because they ascribed properties to rare coins and precious metals which simply are inaccurate.

Let's clear up the confusion.

The first is the belief that one gets wealthy by accumulating money. That is backward thinking. The fact is that one gets wealthy by creating value. Money is only the means of storing the value that has been produced.

The second confusion is mistaking money for investment. Again, this notion is backward. Money — including gold, silver and collectible coins — is not an investment. An investment is something that produces value. If one owns a piece of property and rents it out to get income, owns a share of an enterprise (stock) from which he hopes to profit, or loans money at a fixed rate or return (interest bearing account), he or she has an investment. Gold, silver and rare coins are not investments because they do not produce anything at all let alone anything of value. All they do is store value. In effect, they are savings accounts that generate no interest.

Precisely because they are savings vehicles that store value, gold, silver and rare coins are superb vehicles for trade. The venues in which they are exchanged are called *markets*. At its most basic level, what drives these markets is Economics 101, or to put it another way: supply and demand.

Supply and Demand of Rare Coins and Precious Metals

The supply and demand dynamic works differently for rare coins and precious metals than for most other products. For example, with products like bottled water or paper clips, and almost all consumer items, materials and manufacturing capabilities are sufficient to satisfy any market demand quickly. No matter how high the demand might rise, the supply can easily be increased; or if demand falls, production will be decreased. Except for short-term fluctuations from imbalances in the supply/demand ratio, the result is that prices tend to remain constant over the long term, with a tendency toward the downside as competition and technology nibble away at the cost of production and distribution.

In other markets, such as food and energy, demand is relatively constant, and therefore price changes are driven mainly by the quantity of available supply. If supply is plentiful, producers will drop the price to drive sales. Conversely, if supply is scarce, producers raise prices to insure the ability to obtain new supplies.

What makes gold and silver different is that supply is limited compared with most other elements. If demand increases beyond supply capabilities, prices will rise because producing additional supply is much more difficult and time consuming than it is for most other products. Eventually, prices increase sufficiently to discourage demand, and encourage the creation of more supply, either from production or from people selling gold and silver back into the market (often taking profit on the price increase) causing the price to drop until supply and demand are equalized. Price is the measure and the regulator of the balance between supply and demand. While shortage of supply in the face of higher demand increases prices, an excess of supply in the face of lowered demand decreases prices.

With rare coins, the potential for price increase is even greater because once coins for a certain year are minted, no more coins of that date and denomination will ever be made, which means that the supply of rare coins is not only limited but finite. The only exception is that each year new coins are minted, but this is a relatively slow process.

Furthermore, once supply has been created, it usually is not destroyed, because as we have noted, hard assets like gold, silver and coins are storehouses of value. Thus, unlike food, energy, paper clips or bottled water, which are completely consumed, the supply of coins, gold and, to a lesser extent silver (which is consumed in some industrial uses), will come back into the market if and when demand increases. In fact, massive selling of already produced hard assets is the only way available supply can be rapidly increased. Therefore, the primary factor determining prices for hard assets is demand.

It is not necessary here to get into particulars of how the values of gold or silver, or specific individual coins are impacted by this, as we will explore that later. The crucial point here is to understand the basic dynamic that rare coin and precious metals prices are driven by demand. To fully comprehend how economic and other factors impact the hard asset markets, our key focus must be on the demand side of the equation.

Demand is determined by the aggregate of the intensity and desire of mass numbers of people. People buy or sell for a wide variety of reasons, not all of them logical. Therefore, to understand the dynamics of what causes people to act, we must delve into the psychology of buyers and sellers, especially as it relates to the aggregate of active traders in the marketplace. It becomes useful to know what causes people to buy and sell rare coins and precious metals. The key to unlocking some insight regarding this phenomenon is the concept of *market intelligence*.

Market Intelligence

Market intelligence is the combined knowledge, experience and intuition of everyone who buys or sells in that market. Market intelligence is much more than a mechanism that determines value through supply and demand: it comprises the assimilation of information resources, and the exchange of vast quantities of knowledge. In many ways, it is analogous to a supercomputer that links together the memory and computing power of thousands of computers to accomplish gargantuan tasks that no individual computer could accomplish on its own.

A *Scientific American* article (August, 2009) reported a study showing that if a significant number of people are asked to guess the number of jellybeans in a large jar, the individual guesses will vary widely but the average guess (totaling all the guesses then dividing by the number of participants) is remarkably and surprisingly accurate. That is not a bad analogy to market intelligence. Naturally, market intelligence does not always come to the best conclusion, and it certainly is not foolproof. At times it can be terribly wrong. It does, however, tend to be naturally self-correcting. And in a large free-market environment like the precious metals enjoy, it can self-correct with amazing speed.

Market intelligence operates in areas where large numbers of people buy certain products, which applies to many areas other than rare coins and precious metals. In selecting a movie to see, people make choices using some combination of available data. Some consult reviews (analysis), others look at top box office draws (trading volume), others want the newest horror, thriller or romantic comedy (market sector), and still others look for the latest work of a certain actor, director or writer (collector). All of this decision-making criteria is part of market intelligence.

Even though the various buyers will see a particular movie for different reasons, the number of people who buy tickets is an indication of the desirability of that overall entertainment product, which will be reflected in its revenue. This is the principal reason movie distributors make such a big deal out of box office grosses — it entices more people to come to the same conclusion. It is also why political operatives strive to spin the results of polls to show that their side is winning. It helps with fundraising and getting supportive voters to the polls. It may even discourage some people from going to the polls if they feel their chosen candidate is destined to lose.

This principle operates in the stock market. As buys and sells are recorded — and prices rise and fall accordingly — traders constantly look for imbalances where the supply (from people who want to sell) has caused the price to drop below the stock's true value, thus creating a profit opportunity. To make this determination, traders will analyze a wide variety of fundamental and technical factors.

The same phenomenon operates every day in the rare coin business. The Certified Coin Exchange, an online trading network for professional dealers, provides a venue where members can offer and request coins of all values, along with some non-coin collectible rarities. CCE also trades every kind of precious metal, in all forms, from sterling and bars to coins and scrap.

In addition to prices being offered, dealers can see how many other dealers are looking for a particular item, and contrast that with how many wish to sell that item. This provides an inside look at the balance between sellers and buyers as well as the *spreads*, which indicate the motivational intensity of buyers and sellers. On occasion, dealer comments provide additional insights. Only a small fraction of all dealers are buying or selling on the exchange at any given time, so the information is by no means complete, but it is an interesting slice of extremely useful, valuable information, or intelligence, about the market. The same dynamic occurs, albeit on a more haphazard basis, at coin shows where a concentrated number of dealers and collectors are present.

Market intelligence, therefore, is the underlying, dominating force behind any price trend. It is the primary factor behind economic bubbles of all kinds, from the boom-and-bust cycle of Dutch tulips in the 1600s to the rise and fall of dot-com tech stocks in the 1990s. More recently, astute market watchers would have noted that real estate prices were handily outpacing income levels, and that banks and other financial institutions were making highly questionable loans in the years preceding the housing market debacle of 2008.

The Collector Mentality

The most significant economic factor impacting the rare coin market, which also impacts the precious metals markets in a limited way, is the collector. Understanding the collector's mentality and how it works is essential to understanding the demand dynamic of hard asset markets.

Most hobbies cause people to divest themselves of money: just ask any scuba diver, golfer or boat owner. The nature of coin collecting, whether rare or not, involves the accumulation of money. While accumulating assets is an economic motivation, economics are not always the primary motivation of collectors. For many collectors, the primary motivation is enjoyment. Collectors are motivated by the desire to own certain objects.

Coins are historical. The images and symbols depicted in their designs reveal intriguing insights into historical events, cultural movements and political philosophy. Coins often display portraits of important historical figures. United States coins provide superb examples. Starting in 1909 and continuing to the present, the U.S. cent has displayed the portrait of Abraham Lincoln. Before that, the cent had a portrait of a Native American chief, as a romantic homage to this era of American history. That same romanticism continued with the Buffalo nickel, and continues today with the $1 one-ounce silver Buffalo and the $50 one-ounce gold Buffalo.

Beginning in 1938, the nickel portrayed Thomas Jefferson. From 1948 to the present, Franklin Roosevelt's profile has been on the dime. Since 1932, George Washington's profile has been on the quarter. Between 1948 and 1963, Benjamin Franklin's portrait was on the half dollar. In more modern times, the dollar bore portraits of Eisenhower, Susan B. Anthony, Native American "princess" Sacagawea, and now all the American presidents. Many coins were designed to commemorate important events such as the Columbian Exposition or the San Francisco World's Fair of 1936, and famous people like George Washington Carver or Booker T. Washington.

The same holds true for bank notes, with George Washington on the $1, Lincoln on the $5, Hamilton on the $10, Jackson on the $20, Grant on the $50 and Franklin on the $100. It is interesting to note that the highest denomination note ever made for U.S. Dollars, the $10,000 bank note, features the picture of someone most of us never heard of: Salmon P. Chase, Secretary of the Treasury 1861-64, and later a Supreme Court Justice. Incidentally, $10,000 bank notes, which were primarily used for funds transfers between banks are now worth more than $30,000 in any condition. That is because of collector demand.

United States 1896 Silver Certificates, known as educational banknotes, issued in $1, $2 and $5 denominations, depict neoclassical imagery on the obverses. The reverse of this $2 certificate honors inventors Robert Fulton (left) and Samuel Morse (right). *Image courtesy of the National Numismatic Collection at the Smithsonian Institution*

In some cases, such as with the educational banknotes — silver certificates issued in denominations of $1, $2 and $5 at the end of the 19th century — a deliberate attempt was made to include the names of prominent writers, scientists and historical figures on the banknote itself — hence their denotation as *educational*. It is perhaps not surprising that the educational notes are among the most beautiful banknote designs ever made by the U.S. government.

Beyond purely historical significance is aesthetic enjoyment. Coins and banknotes are miniature works of art, intricately designed, rendered and produced. They are attractive to the eye and despite being mass produced, there are subtle and sometimes not so subtle differences even between coins or notes that were produced at the same time and at the same mint. Many people simply enjoy finding that gem quality example of a particular design, the one with the best luster, the fewest marks, the best strike and a particular look that only an trained eye can appreciate. Or perhaps that one coin that got chewed up in the minting process and has become an error coin or an error banknote. Some people actually make an effort to collect the worse possible condition coin!

Others are enraptured by or have an emotional connection to the figure portrayed on the coin. Shortly after President John F. Kennedy was assassinated, the U.S. mint changed the design of the fifty-cent piece from Benjamin Franklin to John F. Kennedy. When those coins were first minted in 1964, many people were so emotionally connected with JFK that they hoarded those half dollars. As a result, for a long time, they were almost impossible to find in circulation. Eventually the ardor dissipated, and the coins became more available. However — and this is fascinating — so many coins were minted and saved in uncirculated condition that uncirculated 1964 Kennedy half dollars are plentiful today despite the fact that 1964 is the only date when Kennedy halves were minted of 90-percent silver.

There is also the mystique of the rare date or mintmark. The 1916 Mercury dime is a relatively common coin, which in choice, uncirculated condition can be had for less than $100. On the other hand, it would cost at least $10,000 to acquire a 1916-D Mercury dime (the "D" signifying that the coin was minted in Denver) even in barely uncirculated condition. That little "D" makes a huge difference. Why? Because the collector demand for it is much greater than the available supply.

The old U.S. Mint in San Francisco, CA is now on the National Register of Historic Places.

The "D" mintmark can also make a huge difference if found on pre-civil-war era gold coins, as it indicates coins minted in Dahlonega, Georgia. A "C" mintmark from the same era gold is for Charlotte, North Carolina, the "O" mintmark for New Orleans, Louisiana, the "S" mintmark for San Francisco, California, and then, of course, the famous "CC" mintmark for Carson City, Nevada. Many of the modern day commemoratives and other coins are minted at West Point, New York and have a "W" mintmark. Coins with no mintmark were minted in Philadelphia, the main mint.

An interesting side note is that the original San Francisco mint building survived the 1906 earthquake, and as of a few years ago, became the site of the twice-annual San Francisco coin show. There is something truly historic about trading late 1800's San Francisco Mint coins in the same building where they were minted over 100 years ago. Should you ever attend, don't forget to take a building tour, which is absolutely fascinating.

Many collectors make it a goal to collect an example of each and every date and mintmark of a particular coin design. Some such sets are relatively small, such as the Flying Eagle Cent series, a coin that was made from 1856-58 with a total of only four major dates and varieties. Other sets have moderate numbers, like Peace dollars with 24 to 26 coins depending on the varieties included and the gold $2.5 Indians with 15 different dates. The Lincoln cent series, on the other hand, numbers in the hundreds since it was minted in several cities with several different varieties from 1909 through the present day.

All of the above appeal to what I like to call the *collector mentality*. Like all collectibles — everything from ink wells, Beanie Babies and Barbie dolls to toy trains, cigar bands and famous paintings — people collect them because of their fascination, and in some cases obsession with the objects of their quest.

When I was no older than 10, I became fascinated with matchbooks and matchboxes. They were common giveaways in the 1960s and I remember collecting them from every restaurant or establishment where I could find them, eventually accumulating enough to fill a two-gallon fishbowl. For me, they traced a history of all the places I had been. By the age of 12, I became bored with the collection: It did not take long to realize that no one else was interested in them either. No one would buy them. In fact, no one even wanted them when I tried to give them away. Eventually, I just threw them out — so I could start filling the fishbowl with — you guessed it — coins. That was a good thing too, because later as a young adult, I found myself in need of cash and was able to sell my childhood coin collection for about 50 times its original cost.

The story illustrates both the significance and mercurial nature of the demand side regarding the supply and demand equation as well as the effectiveness of coinage as a storehouse of value.

Because a certain percentage of people always seem to enjoy collecting, it stands to reason that the more people there are in the world, the more demand there will be for collectibles. Furthermore, the wealthier people get, the more likely they are to collect various things.

Money of course is one of the most desirable items precisely because it is money — a storehouse of value. This adds to its emotional appeal as a collectible. Those two demographic trends make a good argument that the demand for coins will continue to rise well into the future.

It is important to distinguish the collector mentality from the idea that in order to be a collector, one must be exceptionally knowledgeable. They are two very different things. Many collectors do indeed know a great deal about the coins they collect and adore. Some can recite not only the price history of the coin, or how rare it is in various grades, but also the history behind its design, the political motivations and circumstances which moved the design forward, all the design variations, as well as other detailed and arcane information relating to that particular coin.

The collector mentality, however, does not require a massive amount of knowledge. It simply requires the desire to collect. Nor is extensive knowledge required to be financially successful through collecting coins.

In the early 1980s, I had the good fortune to attend a talk by General Jimmy Doolittle. The name will ring a bell with WWII history buffs, for it was General Doolittle who led the first and very famous allied raid on Tokyo, Japan. After the war, General Doolittle became interested in pattern coins.

Pattern coins are samples of various designs and metallurgic compositions, and are produced to help Mint officials and members of Congress make the final decisions about which coins will be minted or not. With a few exceptions, pattern coins are exceedingly rare, usually in high grade proof, often exceptionally beautiful. Most patterns show designs that were rejected for use on U.S. coinage. Many of these designs are more attractive than some of the designs that were eventually chosen. It is one of the most fascinating areas of numismatics.

Doolittle's collection, which contained many pattern coins had recently sold for around $17 million. He estimated that he had spent perhaps a quarter of a million dollars to purchase his collection, and, in response to a question suggesting that he must have known a great deal about these coins to spend so much, he replied that he never knew that much about pattern coins, except that he liked them and trusted the dealers he was working with would give him a fair deal. If he had the money and liked the look of the coin, he bought it. Doolittle's educated intuition perhaps served him better — at least from a financial perspective — than any specific coin knowledge. Instead of educating himself, he relied on the experience and education of dealers he trusted.

A perfectly fine way to collect coins, General Doolittle's acquisition method illustrates the unpredictable and fickle characteristics of the collector mentality. The reason his collection sold for so much had at least something to do with the attractiveness to other collectors of pattern coins. Collectors might also have been motivated by the desire to own coins that had once belonged to a famous war hero. The crucial point here is that collector demand is not driven primarily by the scarcity of the object but rather by collector demand. Adopting the collector mentality to tap into this demand dynamic is a powerful strategy. With time and practice, it usually pays handsome financial dividends.

Should people stop collecting coins, causing demand to dry up, their value would drop. This is not likely for reasons we have already discussed, specifically increasing wealth and an increasing population of collectors, as well as for economic reasons we will explore later. The capricious nature of collector demand naturally causes coins to move in and out of favor over time. There are exceptions, however, such as when a new cache or hoard of coins is discovered.

In 1960, a brilliant uncirculated 1903-O Morgan Silver Dollar was considered exceptionally rare and sold for around $1,500. It was assumed that almost all of these coins had been melted down as a result of the Pittman Act of 1917. However, in 1963, a government vault was opened, and hundreds of bags — each containing 1,000 silver dollars — were discovered. Most of these were from the Carson City Mint, but a number of the bags contained 1903-O Morgan dollars.

Even today, more than 50 years after their discovery, prices for that coin have not fully recovered, and brilliant uncirculated examples of the 1903-O sell for only around $500.

Usually, however, this phenomenon works in reverse: Coins that were once considered common are suddenly difficult to find. Demand has outstripped supply and prices consequently soar.

The X Factor of Coin Collecting

So many coins have gone up in value so significantly over time that coins are considered by many to be an investment. This is one of those confusions pointed out earlier. To reiterate, coins do not produce a good or service, nor do they produce value of any other sort except insofar as they are vehicles for storing value. Coins increase in value because they become *collectible*, which is to say, because the demand for them increases while the supply remains constant or is reduced gradually through loss and wear. Demand for them might also rise because of economic conditions that affect all commodities. For example, coins that are made of gold, silver or copper may rise and fall in value following the rise and fall in price of the underlying base metals.

Moreover, it is established fact that coins can increase dramatically in value over time. Therefore, instead of calling coins an investment, which we've demonstrated as factually incorrect, perhaps we can say more accurately that coins comprise a savings account with a wild X factor. That X factor is the collectability of coins — what we refer to as *numismatic value*. If one collects enough coins, it is likely their numismatic value will increase because they have become more attractive to more people as a collectible.

Because coins are in fact money — storehouses of value — and because they are often made out of gold, silver and copper — also storehouses of value — they can play a powerful role in preserving wealth and increasing the monetary stability of their owners. The saying "No one ever went broke with a safe deposit box full of gold coins" may not be 100 percent true, but essentially it passes the "common sense" test.

With a proper focus and educated intuition, coin collecting is one of the few hobbies that almost certainly will increase one's net worth over time.

What distinguishes coins (and their cousins, banknotes) from all other collectibles is the intrinsic value of being government sanctioned legal tender. The importance of this cannot be overstated. If one has a cigar band collection (or a matchbook collection), and wishes to sell it, one must find a willing buyer. If a buyer cannot be found, the collection is worthless. In contrast, coins *are* money, and unless they have been demonetized, they have a price floor exactly equal to face value. If one can't find a willing buyer, one can simply spend them.

Even demonetized coins and currency often have collector value. Old coins minted in ancient Greece, Rome, the Byzantine Empire or any number of governments that no longer exist can be readily exchanged for modern forms of money, usually at values much greater than they stored when originally minted. Even in poor condition, it is highly unlikely for an ancient coin to lose its entire numismatic value.

Just as Greek and Roman coins have appreciated far beyond their original value, modern coins can do the same. At one time, the 1916-D Mercury dime that today costs over $10,000 was only worth ten cents. The 1909-S v.d.b. Lincoln cent, which sells for a minimum of several hundred dollars in any condition today was once worth just one cent. The fact that so many coins have increased so significantly in value over time increases the allure of the hobby in general.

Fiat Money

The introduction of fiat money impacts the precious metals and rare coin markets with a completely different dynamic than does the collector. Up until 1913, U.S. government fiat money was essentially non-existent. According to the U.S. Constitution, (Article 1, Section 10, paragraph 1) all money produced by the government was to be made out of, or at least backed by gold or silver. Most of the coins of that time — half dime through one dollar — were made out of silver, with some dollar and larger denominations made out of gold.

The relationship of the dollar to gold and silver also existed for paper money. A $1 silver certificate could be exchanged at any time for one ounce of silver. A $100 gold certificate could be exchanged for five ounces of gold, at the rate of $20 per ounce.

The establishment of the Federal Reserve Bank in 1913 changed things. The history of the Federal Reserve and its impact could fill several books, but it is not necessary for our purposes to explore its history in detail. There are, however, two monumental changes that have had a powerful influence on the hard asset markets as a result of the central bank's establishment.

First, because one of its primary functions was to provide liquidity to banks, the Federal Reserve effectively took over administration of the U.S. money supply, which previously was a Congressional function. Second, because of this control, the Federal Reserve began to issue *fiat dollars*: money without gold or silver backing.

The Federal Reserve thus authorized for itself the ability to print potentially unlimited amounts of money in the form of Federal Reserve notes. Despite the fact they are measured in dollars and deemed to be of equal value, they have no gold or silver backing, Federal Reserve notes are in essence a separate form of currency. As a result, starting in 1913 and continuing until the present, the U.S. dollar has been on a bumpy but continual road of devaluation (compared to gold and silver) as more and more fiat money is released into circulation.

It should be noted that this is not a unique phenomenon. Governments have historically had a monopoly on the minting of coins and the manufacture of currency. When the money of a government is fully and directly backed by a commodity such as gold and silver, like the U.S. Dollar prior to 1913, growth in the money supply is limited by the amount of that commodity which the government possesses. The only way the money supply can increase is through increased production of gold and silver, which generally will also accompany a growing economy producing more goods and services.

Unlike currency backed by gold, silver, copper — or any other commodity for that matter — fiat money has no intrinsic value beyond the paper (or computer blips) it is printed on. Its value depends upon the imprint of the issuing government's authority declaring — and the people accepting — that it has an intrinsic value and on the abililty of the issuing agency or government to collect taxes to back the bonds issued.

While the amount of commodity-backed currency is limited by the supply of those commodities used for backing, the amount of fiat money that can be manufactured is limited only by the will and ability of the government involved to regulate that currency's supply. Theoretically, the potential production of fiat money is unlimited. Naturally, some countries are far more responsible when it comes to printing excess amounts of fiat money than others, and this must always be taken into consideration.

An infamous 1923 German rentenmark. In 1922 the highest denomination was a 50,000 mark banknote, but one year later the highest denomination became 100,000,000,000,000 marks.

If a government issues too little fiat money in relation to its economic activity, the value of its currency will soar. We saw this phenomenon in the U.S. during the 1930s when the Federal Reserve withdrew a significant percentage of fiat dollars from circulation. This was done to protect the value of the dollar following Franklin Roosevelt's executive order of March 9, 1933 that outlawed the private ownership of gold. It worked, at least insofar as protecting the value of the dollar, which was the genesis of the Depression-era expression "cash is king." From that point, the erosion of the value of the dollar was gradual enough so that it appeared to remain relatively stable for decades.

On the other hand, if a government issues too much fiat currency its value will fall, and indeed this is the more common path. History shows many examples of countries that dramatically increased their currency supply when faced with economic upheaval. For governments that wish to spend more than is collected from tax revenues, there is a great temptation to simply turn on the printing presses.

Germany's Weimar Republic printed so much money that the grim joke was it took a wheelbarrow full of cash to buy a loaf of bread. Dictator Robert Mugabe created so many Zimbabwe dollars (printing a $100 *trillion*

In 1923 German hyperflation spiraled out of control to the point that prices doubled every two days. Man, above, uses retenmarks for wallpaper.

dollar banknote) that it lost all value and had to be demonetized. Today, Zimbabwe has no currency of its own, and uses foreign currencies (mostly U.S. dollars) for all domestic transactions.

The important thing to remember is that value of coins, banknotes or any item used like money (such as gold or silver), including fiat currencies, is in large part determined by the economic policy of governments. As of today, there is not a single currency of any country in the world that is backed by gold or silver. Therefore, all currencies now are fiat money.

This would also hold true for so-called *digital currencies* like Bitcoin, which are not created by governmental entities. While these mediums of exchange are in their infancies, and certainly have the potential to be efficient vehicles for trade, the big question is how effective they are at storing value. If they cannot store value, they will eventually lose any effectiveness as a trading vehicle.

Remember the two salient characteristics of gold, silver and coins are that they are vehicles for efficient trade and storing value. Fiat money is even more convenient for trade than gold or silver bullion because it is easier to move around rapidly. However, it is less effective at storing value than gold or silver which is why their values have been continually decreasing relative to gold and silver. The process by which currency loses value is called *inflation*. History shows that when a country embarks upon a path of creating fiat currency, inflation is almost certainly around the corner.

A hedge against inflation is a strong motivation for buyers of rare coins and precious metals in today's market. The fear is that the continuation of a *loose money* policy by the Federal Reserve coupled with a massive and growing U.S. government debt will lead to higher inflation. Instead of holding dollars, they prefer to hold the original storehouses of value: gold, silver and coins.

Inflation

Despite the fact that inflation refers to a drop in the value of the dollar, most people not directly involved with international trade do not experience it as such. We experience inflation as an increase in the price of goods and services. Thus, in an inflationary environment, where the cost of goods rise when compared to the value of the monetary unit, something that costs $100 today might cost $120 next year.

The same thing can happen to real storehouses of value. While it appears that gold and silver are rising in price because it takes more dollars to purchase the same quantity, what is in fact happening is that gold and silver are holding value while the fiat currencies lose value. It may not be a direct 1:1 correlation because there are other factors, such as industrial demand, which may affect metals prices. However, the erosion of the value of fiat dollars along with the market intelligence about where that value is going in the future is the primary factor in the apparent rise of gold and silver.

The value of gold or silver when compared to other commodities has in fact remained relatively constant. People in their 50s today will remember when two candy bars cost a dime, movie tickets were 50 cents and gasoline was 20 cents a gallon. Obviously these items — and virtually everything else — cost a great deal less then than they do today. This is why we often hear economists use the phrase "when measured in 1970's dollars."

Obverse (depicting President Ulysses S. Grant) and reverse of an 1886 U.S. $5 banknote. Silver certificates were in circulation from 1878 to 1964.

And yet, in terms of silver, the value of goods and services has remained remarkably consistent. With silver at $30 per ounce, the .35 ounces of silver in a silver half dollar is worth around $10.50, pretty close to a $12 movie ticket today; a 1950's silver dime has a silver content worth just over $2 today, which is about the price of those same two candy bars. Back then, gas cost around 20 cents per gallon. At $4 per gallon, gas is worth roughly the same in terms of silver then as it is now.

An additional problem with inflation are the various ways in which it is measured. Social Security payments and many governmental salaries and pensions are indexed according to *Cost of Living Adjustment.* COLA strives to measure inflation by selecting the prices for a certain basket of goods and services using a complicated formula that seeks to determine how many dollars are needed to maintain a certain amount of purchasing ability or standard of living for the average person.

While useful for Social Security, pensions and entitlement payments, this way of viewing inflation has serious problems, both of accuracy and adequacy when it comes to understanding how the phenomena of inflation works. Some of these stem from how the basket of goods and services is selected, others from how they are weighted, considering that some items are important for some people but not for others.

However, perhaps the most serious flaw with how the U.S. government measures inflation is that it does not distinguish between *monetary inflation* and *price inflation*. This distinction must be made if one if one is to have a clear picture of economic dynamics today.

Monetary inflation is where the governmental entity prints more money and increases the supply of fiat money. As we have seen, massive printing of money will cause the value of the dollars printed to fall.

A Series 1928 $500 U.S. Gold Certificate. Used as paper currency from 1863 to 1933, existing gold certificates were technically changed to standard legal tender in 1964, with no connection to gold.

Price inflation occurs when the actual cost of goods rise due to non-monetary factors. These might include a sudden increase in market demand, a spike in manufacturing cost from higher worker salaries, energy or material shortages, increased costs for marketing or distribution, or new restrictive governmental regulation. It is possible to have price inflation without monetary inflation. If there is a freeze in Florida that ruins an orange harvest, there would be price inflation on orange juice. The price increase would be caused by adverse climate conditions that impacted the supply of orange used to make orange juice — and has nothing to do with monetary inflation.

Only by making this distinction is it possible to see how extraordinarily deceptive the commonly accepted perception of inflation is. Official government measures show inflation to be low, averaging just over 2 percent a year for the last 12 years — for a total of 25 percent in that time frame. And yet, gold and silver prices are up 400 to 500 percent over the same period. The inconsistency is revealed as soon as we realize that price deflation is effectively hiding monetary inflation. Here's how it works:

A sluggish economy and high unemployment coupled with strong fears about the future has reduced demand for goods and services across virtually every sector of the economy. People with resources "pull in their horns" and "hunker down," preserving their stored value (money) for potentially even worse times to come; those with limited resources cut back spending at every opportunity. Reduced demand throughout the economy drives prices down, creating *price deflation*.

Meanwhile, massive printing of fiat currency by the U.S. government and the Federal Reserve creates monetary inflation which creates a counterbalance. The U.S. Dollar is not backed, and therefore printing more of them reduces the value of each fiat dollar. Thus, we have monetary inflation and price deflation occurring at the same time. The way the government measures inflation, price deflation due to lower demand for goods and services averages out against monetary inflation due to money printing, making it appear that inflation is low.

Unfortunately, the massive increase in the number of fiat dollars must eventually result in higher prices — first for every day commodities like fuel and food where a consistent demand forces continued production, and later for all other produced commodities and consumer items. However, this degradation in the value of the dollar will not show up in Uncle Sam's inflation figures as long as the economy remains sluggish.

The dollar is degrading nonetheless.

Should the economy heat up, price deflation would reverse itself because in a stronger economy, more people spend more money on more goods and services, and the increased demand will cause price inflation. Because there has been such a vast expansion in the money supply, even more dollars will be needed to purchase the higher priced food, energy and other commodities. Instead of averaging out with monetary inflation, price inflation would combine with monetary inflation, which could lead to serious inflation.

In addition to the new fiat dollars which have already made their way into the economy through federal borrowing and quantitative easing, literally trillions of additional dollars were loaned by the Fed to foreign governments and financial institutions. These dollars have not yet found their way into our economy. But eventually they will, and the weaker the dollar gets, and the higher and more unstable the federal debt becomes, the faster this will happen. Depending on how many new trillions were actually created, how many trillions were already in reserve in those foreign banks, and how many additional trillions will be created in the future to finance our increasing national debt, the end result could be hyperinflation.

Many buyers of hard assets believe that enough new money has already been printed such that hyperinflation is inevitable, and that the only question is when it will happen. Others only see inevitable inflation happening for a long time to come. Where do you think the dollar will be 20 years from now?

The understanding of fiat money and inflation is crucial when it comes to understanding the economic reasons why people buy gold, silver and coins in today's economy. Forty years ago, only a few people spoke passionately about the dangers of fiat money. That number has been gradually increasing, and over the last decade awareness of the issue is widespread. Discussions of the danger posed by the nearly $17 trillion national debt and the fiat dollars used to finance it are not only commonplace in political and business circles, but are now taking place in the mainstream media and around office water coolers in every town across the country. One might say that market intelligence is increasingly aware of the untenable path of current government economic policies.

If there was no such thing as fiat money, this discussion would not be necessary at all, because gold, silver and coins would be the actual money. There would be no fluctuation of hard assets against the value of the dollar because they would be the dollar. We still would be concerned with coins as a collectible, but all economic issues not directly relating to the collectible nature of coins would essentially be moot.

A few miscellaneous facts should be noted.

Generally speaking, we think of the precious metals market as being separate from the rare coin market. This is because gold and silver have no collectible value, only bullion value. Thus, while gold and silver prices will be very sensitive to the strength of the fiat currency, coin prices, at least of the collectible variety are not. However, there is a grey area between the two markets. Many coins are made out of gold and silver, some of which derive most of their value from their gold or silver content. As a result, those coins are also very sensitive to the strength of the fiat currency. This tends to affect the entire coin market. While the two markets are separate, they are also blended, so that frequently — but not always — what affects the bullion markets also affects the coin market, and it may affect different parts of the coin market in different ways.

Between 2008 and 2013, there was such a strong demand for gold that the price jumped from under $800 to over $1600 per ounce. Coin collectors were among those who helped create that demand. To buy more gold and silver, coin buyers bought fewer collectible coins, with the result that many collectible coins held value or went down in value even while gold and silver skyrocketed in value. However, because of their gold content, prices for the more common $20 gold coins, each of which contains nearly an ounce of gold, jumped up in price right along with the price of gold.

So, when we think of these two markets, it is useful to think of them both as separate markets, and as a blended market. To simplify the terminology, the two markets are collectively referred to as the *hard asset* market — terminology used extensively in this book.

Another important fact to keep in mind when discussing the expansion or contraction of the money supply is that most fiat dollars exist only as electronic blips, not as printed banknotes. This makes them an amazingly efficient vehicle for trade. One click of a mouse or scan of a bar code can send millions of dollars to almost anywhere in the world with blazing speed. It also increases the potential for devastating electronic glitches in the financial system. It is ironic that fiat dollars have become the main trading vehicle for gold, silver and rare coins.

It is also important to keep in mind that since all major world currencies are now fiat currencies, there exists the potential for a currency war. A government could print massive amounts of its own currency, or otherwise lower the value of its currency through decree (like China) in order to make their exports more attractive to other countries. However, the four most dominant currencies, the Dollar, the Yen (until recently), the British Pound and the Euro have found it useful to inflate their currencies at roughly the same rate. This keeps their currencies trading among each other at relatively consistent levels, and significantly mitigates the potential for a currency war.

Precious Metals, Rare Coins and the Economy

The rare coin and precious metals markets are only two small components among thousands which, when combined with all other economic activity, comprise the economy. Since the economy involves virtually everyone and everything we buy, sell or barter, how is it possible to calculate its overall effect on only a couple of its miniscule component market parts? Fortunately, that is not necessary for our purposes, because as has been emphasized and will continue to be emphasized, rare coins and precious metals are only involved in the economy as vehicles of trade and storehouses of value, which are essentially passive. Therefore, we can narrow our view to those issues which impact the value hard assets actually store, and in this case, the relevant issue is fiat dollars, with collectability added as an issue for rare coins.

Economic and political landscapes constantly change. It is not necessary for most people to spend a great deal of time or energy on a daily basis the way professionals must, but keeping abreast of important economic and political developments is valuable to anyone who buys, sells or owns rare coins and precious metals. Even more important is to understand the long-term dynamic of these factors.

Background to Current Political and Economic Climate

The strong increase in gold and silver prices since their 1999 lows is the result of buyers reacting to an unprecedented printing of dollars by the Federal Reserve. Since Rep. Ron Paul was unsuccessful in getting a bill passed to audit the Federal Reserve before he retired from the House of Representatives, there are no firm figures about exactly how many dollars the Fed has printed. Indeed, the Federal Reserve stopped publishing money supply figures as of 2006.

What we do know is that money printing has been rampant ever since the September 11, 2001 terrorist attacks. At first, part of this loose monetary policy was an attempt to prevent a recession after the tragic events of that day. By lowering interest rates, the Federal Reserve made it easy for banks to obtain whatever amount of cash they needed, which they were then able to loan out at low rates. This influx of cash or *liquidity* into the economy provided a short-term stimulus that staved off a recession. Yet, instead of keeping the stimulus short term, the Fed continued to keep interest rates extremely low, which pumped additional liquidity into the markets, and, coupled with the Community Redevelopment Act of 1999, a great amount of that liquidity went into the real estate market.

The purpose of the 1999 CRA legislation was to assist more people into homeownership. However, beneath the altruistic sheen, the net effect forced banks into loaning money to unqualified borrowers. In essence, it was a subsidy to the housing market. To entice the banks to go along with this scheme, Freddie Mac and Fannie Mae agreed to purchase these loans and absorb the risk. Since their own capital was not at risk, and since they could profit from every loan they sold, banks and other lending institutions aggressively loaned money with relatively little attention to the real ability of the borrowers to pay back the loans.

This put Uncle Sam — or more specifically the taxpayers — in the position of guaranteeing the loans.

Fannie and Freddie then packaged those mortgage loans and sold them to Wall Street as investments. Senior management at Freddie and Fannie made millions of dollars personally through this mechanism. Because of the semi-official relationship between the federal government and Fannie and Freddie, Wall Street was able, with a wink and a nod, to claim that these mortgage-backed securities were insured by the federal government. That sales pitch made them very attractive to investors, who generally glanced at the rating companies' favorable analysis and accepted that these securities were safe.

As housing prices escalated, and homeowners began taking on second mortgages – essentially using their houses as ATMs – the equity in those homes, which was the protection for the investors, started to dissipate. This worked sufficiently well so long as house values rose, but when the housing bubble burst, many homeowners found themselves underwater on their loans.

Meanwhile, some of the shaper pencils on Wall Street realized that the home mortgage security market was out of balance and would likely collapse. Betting against the value of securities using Collateralized Debt Obligations and other insurance instruments, they made a fortune when the housing market crashed while those who owned the actual securities, which included a lot of banks, investment firms and other entities, including individuals, lost massively.

To prevent the larger banks and insurance behemoths, like AIG — deemed "too big to fail" — which had bet heavily on these securities from going bankrupt, the U.S. government's Troubled Asset Relief Program was instituted. The bailout capital was provided by additional U.S. government borrowing. New fiat dollars flooded the market, not only to prevent a recession as had been the case earlier in the decade, but to prevent a total collapse of the U.S. banking system.

European banks, governments and investors were also impacted, and, unbeknownst to most of the American people, the Federal Reserve loaned huge sums to many of those foreign institutions. Specific figures about how many fiat dollars were created were not made public, so it is impossible to say with certainty exactly how much, but usually reliable sources estimate a range from $15 to $24 trillion.

It gets worse.

To insure they could flood the system with liquidity, the Fed lowered the interest rate to near-zero percent. This insured that the borrowing institutions could absorb the capital with almost no cost, shoring up their capital reserves. It was the announced hope that this infusion of capital would boost the economy, which had just begun a serious recession.

But the dragon of unintended consequences let loose a fireball.

Silver options trading pit at the Commodity Exchange in New York.
Photo courtesy David Mark

Despite low interest rates, instead of making loans available to businesses and homebuyers, which would stimulate the economy, the banks bought Treasury bonds. It made monetary sense: The banks were borrowing money from the Fed at close to zero interest, which they used to buy treasuries that paid around 3 percent. In essence, they made interest on money that costs them nothing to borrow. It's like "money for nothing" — similar to what some of us did with credit cards prior to 2008, when we took out balance transfers at zero percent, then deposited that money into an interest bearing account at a bank.

Buying treasuries had the additional advantage of augmenting the cash reserves of those banks, thereby strengthening their weakened balance sheets.

Much to the government's chagrin, the banks had no incentive to loan that money to businesses. Why take a risk on a low rate business loan when risk-free Treasury bonds at 3 percent are available? In essence, the banks borrowed as much as they possibly could from the Fed, then turned right around and loaned it (back) to the U.S. government, pocketing the spread between interest rates. What was meant to stimulate the economy actually had the opposite effect.

Government stimulus money was not used to buy inventory, build businesses, or create goods and services. Only a small fraction was used for infrastructure. Much of it was diverted to fund federal budget obligations, including welfare and other entitlement programs.

With the government inadvertently quashing liquidity, and the passage of ill-conceived banking legislation like Dodd-Frank, it became extremely difficult for businesses — even well-established, solid companies — to borrow money. The economy has been in the doldrums ever since.

What was a bad situation under the Bush administration has become much worse under Obama. Since 2008, federal spending has skyrocketed from about $2.5 trillion to nearly $4 trillion per year. Tax revenues remained relatively flat, so Uncle Sam borrowed even more money to pay the bills, posting the first annual deficit of over $1 trillion dollars in U.S. history. The annual deficit has not gone below $1 trillion until this year, but even the most optimistic predictions do not project that the federal budget will balance anytime within the next decade. Depending on how out of control as of yet unknown costs of Obamacare and other programs become, the federal debt could possibly exceed $20 trillion by the time President Obama leaves office and could approach the $30-trillion level by 2025.

Normally, when massive quantities of fiat dollars are printed, they go into the economy to fund business development, which provides a short-term stimulus to the economy that in turn produces value in the form of goods and services. The cost of that stimulus is inflation of the currency.

Instead, this increased liquidity was primarily used to fund U.S. government obligations, and as a consequence economic growth has been relatively flat. Thus, not only has government policy failed to create a dynamic that could produce a strong economy, but it has created massive monetary inflation masked by price deflation. The perils of monetary inflation, the dynamic of which *is* in place, awaits in the future like a Category 5 hurricane on the radar screen.

Exacerbating the situation, the Federal Reserve has committed to quantitative easing at the rate of $85 billion per month, which totals about $1 trillion per year. Fed Chairman Bernanke has stated that quantitative easing will remain in place until the unemployment rate reaches around 6.5 percent. Although recent jobs reports have shown some signs of a recovery, even the most optimistic forecasts indicate that it will take years before we see 6.5-percent unemployment again.

Not only does an expansionary monetary policy push more cash into government debt, but the long-run effect is inflationary. Should interest rates be allowed to rise, the interest cost on the ever growing federal debt would soon become the largest item in the United States budget. That could potentially destabilize the U.S. economy. Thus, the Fed is forced to continue its current policy of doing its best to keep the house of cards intact. Hopefully they will succeed and the economy will start to grow. This is unlikely, however, because while quantitative easing might give a temporary boost to economic activity, it cannot — as we have seen over the last five years — initiate economic recovery by itself.

Ironically, the erosion of the dollar produces an interesting upside: It reduces the value of the U.S. debt. After all, if the U.S. government owes $17 trillion dollars, and the dollar falls by, say, 50 percent, then the actual asset value of the debt falls by the same 50 percent, and entities that own U.S. debt — like the Chinese government — will eventually find the value of their investment in U.S. dollars dropping precipitously.

Before jumping up with a cheer — yes, the Chinese have been playing hardball currency manipulation for years — it would be wise to remember that the process that reduces the value of the dollar also affects everyone else who holds U.S. government debt. In addition to governments like China and many European countries and corporations who have purchased U.S. government debt, the declining value of the dollar hurts pensioners who own U.S. government debt. The Social Security Trust Fund, which by law must be invested in U.S. government bonds and is already rooted in shaky financial ground, could be forced to reduce benefits, placing additional hardships on the country's retirees. It also hurts individual Americans who have been saving cash for their retirement, because that cash will be worth a lot less by the time they need to use it.

A falling dollar also reduces the value of pensions for government workers, much of which is currently *unfunded,* meaning not enough money has been put away to cover expected future expenditures. What will happen if there is not enough money in the future to cover these expenses?

Those with a cynical or ideologically ignorant perspective would say that to cover these expenses all the government has to do is authorize the printing of more money. While that might allow the government to cover the actual dollar count of what is owed, the value of those dollars would continually be reduced depending on how many were printed. The net result is that despite remitting the same actual number of dollars, the purchasing value of each dollar would be much less in the future, meaning a lower standard of living for the pensioners.

It is important to bear in mind that this is not just an economic cost. There is also a large human cost. The people who would be most affected by a fall in the value of the dollar are the poor and anyone else who lives hand-to-mouth. Salaries and pensions rise more slowly than other economic sectors, so every drop in the value of the dollar translates into a real drop in their standard of living.

Other people likely to suffer are the elderly and the baby boomers, who will enter that demographic in the next ten to fifteen years. These are people who saved all their lives for a comfortable retirement, but may find themselves running out of money as low interest rates and a devaluating dollar prevents them from living off their portfolio earnings, forcing them to live off the principal sooner than they had planned. It is for this reason that Nobel Prize economist Milton Friedman called inflation the "cruelest tax" of all.

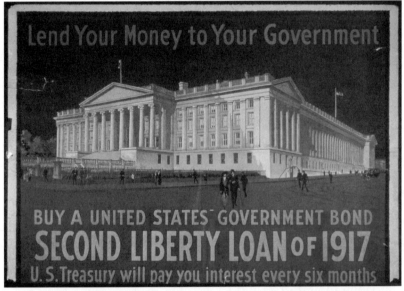

Social Security funds must be invested in U.S. government bonds — rather than assets invested in wealth producing instruments. Government bonds are secured by the ability of the federal government to collect tax revenues. As taxpayers, in a sense, we are paying the interest on our own investment in Social Security.

The Pension Bomb

Based on all responsible financial projections, federal government revenues will fall short of what is required to pay future obligations for such programs as Social Security, Medicare, the Affordable Health Care Act, federal pensions and other entitlement programs.

It is difficult if not impossible to predict exactly what these costs will be. Some of the most important issues involved in this determination, which include ever-changing government tax and spend policies, economic conditions, medical advances, human psychology and demographic trends are exceedingly complex. The numbers necessary to calculate the economic impact are large and unwieldy.

These unfunded liabilities — meaning the projected shortfall of funds necessary to pay for the retirement, pension and health costs for people now in the system — are a major potential problem. Estimates of the total unfunded liabilities range from $50 to 70 trillion dollars on the low side to as much as $150 trillion or more on the high side.

The pension bomb is also ticking for state and local governments, and threatens to bankrupt states such as Illinois, California and New York, with others not far behind. Even with reform, pension obligations in many states and major cities could exceed 50 to 70 percent of some state and local budgets within just a few years. San Diego, CA is already at that level. Several cities around the country have declared bankruptcy because of pension costs. Most recently, Detroit, MI has joined this club.

While many of these obligations are on the state or local level, the fear — not completely unfounded by any means — is the possibility that the federal government could be called upon to bail out states and cities to keep their pension funds solvent, which would place an additional burden at the federal level.

What Does the Future Hold?

One of the serious impediments in predicting future trends is that much of what impacts the economy is increasingly determined by government. As a consequence of an economy that is increasingly influenced by political rather than market-driven forces, there are relatively fewer people making the decisions that impact the masses — decisions that are made according to political calculus rather than market calculus. Market forces still operate, but the ability for companies to react in a dynamic business environment is hampered by a certain amount of political resistance.

Looking ahead for the economy, there are perhaps three possible paths. First is what we might call the Calvin Coolidge approach, which rapidly pulled the U.S. out of a recession into strong economic growth in the early 1920s. It would require drastic cuts in federal spending, significant entitlement reform, a flatter tax code, rapid increase in energy production, a balanced federal budget and significant changes or elimination of key pieces of legislation like Dodd-Frank and the Affordable Health Care Act. Such a path would stimulate economic growth, encourage trillions of dollars now on the sidelines into the economy and increase tax revenue.

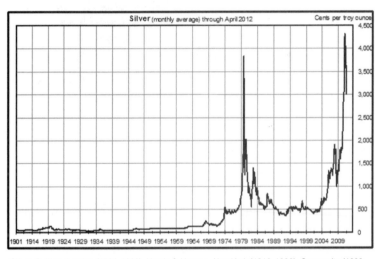

Silver: Bullion, London (1901-1909); Handy & Harman, New York (1910-1990); Composite (1990-date). *Chart courtesy Commodity Research Bureau*

A possible downside of this economic growth could be price inflation, which would dovetail with the monetary inflation that has already been created. But then, too, the Fed would likely pull back on the reins, slowing the growth of the money supply, and the national debt may even start to fall — all of which would be good for economic stability. While higher interest rates would have different effects on different sectors of the economy, for precious metals it typically translates to higher prices. Possibly much higher. As storehouses of value, rare coins and precious metals are an important hedge against monetary inflation.

The second path, one that is much more probable, is that we will continue with current policies. The trend of a substantive government presence in business affairs, a minimal restructuring of entitlement programs, and a tax policy that favors rate hikes would likely cause the economy to remain sluggish.

A rising federal debt would require additional easing of the money supply, which is, in effect, the current Federal Reserve policy. More debt, or *reserve inflation*, will build up, increasing the danger of a currency collapse or crisis. Should this include some measure of economic recovery, such as might result from significantly increased energy production, interest rates would rise along with price inflation, which could propel the hard asset markets upward significantly. While this path could be maintained for some time, eventually it will break down into either the first path or the following one.

The third path is where the federal government truly overshoots, borrowing and spending well beyond its means. The aftermath of an imprudent stimulus package that includes the printing of additional trillions would set the stage for people to lose confidence in the value of the dollar. Inflation could turn serious, leading to hyperinflation or worse. People could stop accepting the dollar as a means of exchange.

As long as the policies and conditions driving down the dollar continue, the upward trend for gold, silver and rare coins will likely remain in place. While unlikely, the worst case scenario would be a complete collapse of the monetary system, which is unlikely but not out of the realm of possibility.

Even if financial Armageddon is never fully realized, the economic climate is ripe for some measure of inflation. Current economic realities and governmental monetary policy make all but certain that the value of the dollar will continue to drop long into the future.

No matter which of these paths the country follows, the inexcapable conclusion is that it makes sense to own gold, silver and rare coins as a hedge against the troublesome signposts in the economy. The only remaining questions are "How much?" and "In what form?"

Chapter One

Where to Begin

THIS CHAPTER IS DESIGNED TO ENCOURAGE you to examine the macro view of your own economics. While this may be unnecessary for some, especially collectors, it is much more important for people whose interests are investment oriented. Investments generally have the goal of increasing value or security. And while technically speaking, rare coins and precious metals are not investments, there is no doubt that in a world dominated by fiat dollars, they sometimes look and even act like investments. The questions posed in this chapter are designed as a guide to enable you to achieve the goals that are most important to you.

The place to begin is the place where you are. Although some people have a good idea as to where they stand with regard to their assets, most only have a vague or an inaccurate idea.

As a reader, it can be assumed that if you do not already own hard assets, you are thinking about it. One of the major goals of this book is to give you the tools to determine the best course of action to meet your specific needs.

What Color are *Your* Assets?

Some years ago, I taught a course at the Learning Annex (based on my e-book *Balance Transfer Magic*) teaching people effective strategies to reduce and pay off their credit card debt utilizing low interest rate balance transfers and requiring only their current income. The first step was for each student to make two lists: one of their debts and another of their assets.

As a general rule most people had a good idea of how much they owed. In a class about debt that was not surprising. What was surprising, however, was the overwhelming majority had no clear idea of their assets. When asked to guess, their guesses turned out to be shockingly inaccurate. In almost every case, they discovered they owned far more than they ever thought possible.

In the world of rare coins and precious metals, owning assets is the name of the game. Focusing on your assets therefore, whether already owned or which you desire to own, is the key to coming out on top.

Before contemplating what assets you desire, it makes sense to find out what assets you already own. To do that, make a Chart of Assets. Since our focus is on hard assets, the chart on the opposite page devotes more detail to those areas. Nevertheless, it is important to also include other monetary assets, because that knowledge will prove essential in revealing what additional resources are available to convert to hard assets should you choose to do so.

For purposes of this exercise, a general idea of total value of each asset is sufficient. Collector coins can be listed in a variety of ways, though I suggest to simply divide your coins into categories: rarities, bullion coins, generic gold and low value collectibles, and give the approximate value totals for each category.

The idea here is to get an overall picture of your financial position, especially relative to any precious metals and coins already owned. For example, one might have a 100-ounce bar of silver, three 10-ounce bars of silver, and 24 one-ounce silver rounds. These can be listed separately, but listing them as "154 oz. silver bullion" is easier and sufficient for our purposes.

Once every item or class of items is listed, place a monetary value on those items and total each line. Again, the monetary value need not be precise to the penny, or even to the dollar, because our intention is to develop an overview. Thus, if silver is $34.25 an ounce, calculating the

Sample **Chart of Assets:**

Asset	Quality	Value/Unit	Quantity	Hard Asset	Current Value
1. Gold					
a. 1 oz Krugerand	Circulated	$1,500	7	$ 10,500	$ 10,500
b. Jewelry scrap	14k	.5 of spot	4 oz	3,400	3,400
2. Silver					
a. 100 oz bar	.999	$32	2	6,400	6,400
b. 1 oz Silver Eagle	Pure	$32	300	9,600	9,600
c. 90% silver*	$ .10, .25, .50	.715 of spot	$140 FV	3,200	3,200
3. Numismatics					
a. $20 St Gaudens	MS-65	$2,250	2	4,500	4,500
b. 1881-S Morgan	MS-65	$160	10	1,600	1,600
c. Mint & proof sets	New	Varies	14	160	160
4. Cash					
a. B of A	CD				75,000
b. Citibank	CD				40,000
5. Stocks & Bonds					
a. Scott Trade	Personal				375,000
b. Ameritrade	IRA				235,000
6. Real estate					
a. Home	Equity				426,000
b. Rental	Equity				170,000
7. Insurance					
a. Whole life					34,000
8. Art	Various				20,000
9. Cars					
a. Jaguar XKE	Needs Wk				16,000
10. Misc					25,000
			Total(s):	$ 39,360	$1,455,360

Hard assests as a percentage of total assets: 2.7%

*A handy formula for 90% bags of silver (aka junk silver): Face Value x .715 x Spot Price = Current Melt Value

49

current value by using $34 or $35 will work equally well. If the current value of an asset is not known or cannot readily be obtained, leave it blank for now.

As a general rule, financial planners recommend that somewhere between 5 to 20 percent of a person's investment portfolio be in hard assets. Because of the recent climb of gold and silver, and the strong likelihood that prices will continue to rise over the next few years, many financial planners advise holdings much closer to the 20 percent than the 5 percent. Some suggest more, some suggest less. Each person is different and the amount one should put into hard assets will vary depending on an individual's situation and goals. Making this list of assets will provide valuable information toward that end.

Defining your Motives, Goals and Needs

After finishing the Chart of Assets, the next step is to determine if you have sufficient hard assets for your needs. But before taking action, it is a good idea to take a few minutes to address issues that likely will come up as you begin to assemble a hard asset portfolio.

It is useful to answer the following questions. I suggest approaching this as a work in progress, subject to change as time goes on, and as you learn more about the hard asset arena.

- Is this for investment only, or do I wish to have some fun with it?
- What percentage of my assets do I want to put into this area?
- Do I have the liquid cash necessary to achieve the above percentage figure?
- How important, on a scale of one to 10 is instant liquidity?
- In what form do I want to have my hard assests?
- Do I want physical possession, or do I want a third party to store my hard assets?
- If I take physical possession, where will I keep it?
- When do I plan to sell?
- What methods will I use to sell?

- Do I plan to pass these assets to my heirs?
- Is this for long-term financial security, or do I hope to make a fast profit?
- On a scale of one to 10, what is my risk tolerance level?

Writing down additional notes and thoughts during this process is highly recommended. Additional questions might arise during this process, or there might be specific issues that these questions do not address. Yet these are typically the most important ones, and answering them will facilitate achieving your goals and avoiding costly mistakes.

Determining Time Horizons

There are two important questions relating to the time horizon. First is determining the deadline by which you intend to assemble the core of your hard asset portfolio. Collectors likely have no deadline at all, and may be purchasing desired coins as they can be found. Diehard collectors often continue their pursuit for the rest of their lives.

On the other hand, those who are investment oriented might prefer to make a strong and relatively rapid diversification into hard assets — before precious metals or coin prices climb even higher. Or perhaps the goal is to gradually accumulate a hard asset portfolio at a rate of a certain number of dollars per year. Keep in mind that no one formula is ideal for everyone: Find the method that most closely fits your specific needs, temperament and capabilities.

The second time horizon is the length of time you intend to hold the hard asset portfolio before selling. Let's say you plan to buy a house in three years and will need all possible liquid assets for that purpose. In the meantime, you decide to hold that liquidity in the form of hard assets. It would almost certainly make more sense to purchase bullion rather than rarities. On the other hand, if the plan is to hold your hard assets for 20 years or more, it would make sense to snatch up a few choice rarities while prices are still low.

If your goal is to assemble a $100,000 portfolio between now and the end of the year, as opposed to building a $100,000 portfolio over

10 years by allocating $10,000 per annum, your plan of attack ought to be adjusted accordingly. Instead of relatively inexpensive semi-numismatic coins, perhaps your time is better spent acquiring rare Reconstruction-era branch mint gold pieces.

Age is also an important factor to consider. A 60-year-old man who wants to shift assets to protect his retirement and cash positions will have a markedly different plan as compared to a 35-year-old who has decided upon an altogether more aggressive hard asset portfolio strategy.

Again, there is no right answer for every one. Financial crisis is often borne out of making decisions that are fundamentally in conflict with your goals. Knowing your goals and putting down on paper a path of how to get there will provide you with an invaluable edge with regard to your eventual outcome. A predetermined plan will give you added confidence when it comes to actual purchasing.

Your time horizons may change, but knowing what they are now is important when considering what kinds of coins and precious metals to buy, and how to go about buying them.

Chapter Two

Ways and Means of Buying and Selling

THERE ARE MANY WAYS TO BUY AND SELL gold, silver and rare coins. No single method is perfect for everyone, nor is there a single method that is best for all occasions. What methods are best for you will depend on three basic factors:

- Do you wish to take physical possession?
- Bullion or rare coins?
- Are you the buyer or seller?

Physical Possession: Take It or Leave It

Rare coins are always a physical possession item. While changes in the sophistication of storage facilities, certified bar coding, advanced photography and other technological advances may cause this to change in the future, as of 2013, the only reliable way to own rare coins is to take physical possession of them. Therefore, the choice about whether or not to take physical possession applies only to gold and silver bullion.

The main advantages of taking physical possession are having complete control over the assets and immediate access at all times. There is a certain comfort that comes from holding gold and silver in your hands. Having physical possession eliminates any concern about the integrity of other people who might be holding your hard assets, or to have to wait if the holding facility is not open at the time you desire access.

The main disadvantages of taking physical possession are the added expenses involved, which typically include delivery, storage and security costs — all of which require some time and effort to get into place. Trading bullion electronically, whether via bank certificates or an exchange, generally enjoys lower commissions, and orders can be executed in the blink of an eye.

At the same time, gold and silver assets held in this way will not quickly or easily be available in an emergency. This is especially true if trading in the electronic markets were halted or interrupted due to national emergency or cyber attack.

This is not an all or nothing choice. Many people own a silver exchange-traded fund and also have physical possession of gold coins. An ETF enables them to speculate on the price of silver, while holding physical possession of gold provides the comfort and security of instant access.

If arranging for secure storage is not possible for whatever reason, paper possession may be the only realistic choice. The obvious reason for this is that physical items are subject to theft and loss, and if they are not stored with adequate care and safeguards, these assets are in danger of "disappearing."

Paper possession can also be useful for the elderly, infirm or frequent traveler who does not want to bother with having to find secure storage for their precious metals. This is particularly true for silver, because of its sheer physical weight and volume, but not so much for gold. At today's prices, $100,000 in gold weighs less than five pounds, and can easily be carried in a purse, briefcase, backpack or stored in a small safe deposit box. The same value in silver weighs close to 300 pounds and would fill a large safe or several safe deposit boxes. It is easy to see why so many seniors trade their silver for gold and numismatic coins.

Paper possession requires other entities to store your precious metals. While most companies and vaulting facilities do this safely and effectively, problems can and do occur. One of the more glaring and well publicized examples in recent years relates to MF Global, the financial conglomerate once headed up by former New Jersey Governor

John Corzine. Once considered to be a company of highest integrity, MF Global held gold in trust for their customers and issued warehouse receipts, and then pledged that gold as collateral for other trades. As outrageously unfair as it may be, because of the contract terms of those warehouse receipts, it is possible that these customers of MF Global will lose their holdings.

In addition to individuals, paper assets that control physical metals are frequently used either by companies whose business is impacted by precious metals prices, or by traders who are looking to generate short term profits. In the area of precious metals these kinds of paper assets present unique risks. Any investor or speculator who uses these methods, or is thinking of using these methods, should research thoroughly not only the method itself, but the contracts and the contracting entities involved, and then proceed with caution.

Exchange and Related Trading Vehicles

Mining stocks, ETFs, commodity exchanges and IRAs — each with pros and cons — are the most common methods of participating in the precious metals markets without taking physical possession.

Mining stock prices tend to rise and fall along with the prices of precious metals those companies produce. However, mining stocks are shares in a company and as such they are dependent on factors that affect all stocks, including management philosophy, strategy, personnel, capitalization, contractual agreements, governmental regulations, environmental hazards, profit margin and so forth. Because there are dozens of well-known mining companies, foreign and domestic, different rules for each state and country must also be taken into account.

It is recommended that the same kind of caution and research be applied as one would use before investing in any stock. Generally speaking, the people who buy mining stocks are experienced stock investors.

Exchange-traded funds are a relatively new way to own gold, silver and other precious metals. The value of an ETF is directly related to the price of the precious metal involved. Thus, a gold ETF will increase in value if gold prices go up, and will fall if gold prices go down.

ETFs are designed such that commissions on trades are low or non-existent, and moving funds in and out is rapid, simple and executed electronically. This is one of the most popular ways to own gold or silver. It is a particularly useful method for speculators, day traders and others who want to be able to sell quickly — especially if they are chasing quick profits based on short-term fluctuations. This form of ownership also might be ideal for someone who knows they will need cash for other needs in a relatively short time frame.

Don't be confused, though. ETFs are not the same as owning physical gold or silver. In fact, an ETF is an investment fund that holds an asset like gold or silver — often in the form of a contract — and trades at a price that reflects its net asset value. Contractually, ETFs are obligated to own sufficient contracts to cover the quantity of gold represented by all the purchasers of the fund. This presents a potential problem. From time to time, doubts have surfaced about whether some ETFs have had sufficient backing to cover the shares they sold or the contracts they hold. Should there be any kind of market collapse, or if some of those contracts cannot be filled due to factors as diverse as war, political unrest, economic collapse or natural disaster, there is a danger these funds would simply not pay out. Ironically, these are some of the same circumstances under which the price of precious metals would be expected to soar. So, before buying ETFs, get educated about them with special attention paid to the risks involved.

Commodity futures and options were originally designed to enable companies that use a generic commodity like corn or silver to protect themselves against adverse future price fluctuations.

If a company is a supplier of precious metals to industry, and, say, recently purchased a large quantity of gold, they may wish to take a short position in gold to protect against a drop in market price. Conversely, a manufacturing concern that uses silver in their process may wish to take a long position of silver futures contracts to protect their supply price against a future upward spike. These strategies are common in other industries as well. Airlines frequently buy oil futures to protect against dramatic increases in the price of fuel, and farmers sell futures to guarantee a fixed price for their harvest to protect against precipitous drop in market prices for the crops they grow.

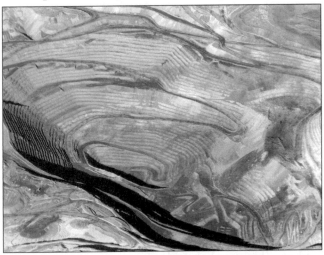

Round Mountain gold mine in Nevada is a joint venture of Kinross Gold and Barrick Gold. The open pit mine originally started out as an underground mining operation in 1906 and produced 350,000 ounces of gold over a 60-year period. It is interesting to note that while there are many gold mining operations, silver is usually produced as a byproduct of other mineral mining interests. *Aerial photo by Patrck Huber*

For precious metals investors, futures contracts are an extremely efficient and convenient way to take delivery — but only for those in need of large quantities. One Comex gold contract is 100 ounces, which translates to a terrific amount of money for most people. If one does take delivery of a futures contract, commissions are low — usually a double commission plus delivery and, if necessary, storage fees. Of course, as soon as physical delivery is made, it is no longer a paper asset and it now crosses into the category of physical ownership.

Some people purchase options and futures not to protect their companies' commodity interests or to take delivery, but rather as speculative financial instruments. The futures markets offer traders a tremendous amount of leverage through the use of what is called a *margin requirement*. Put up $1 to control, say, $10 or $20 worth of a commodity. This is both the brilliant *and* the terrifying aspect of futures trading. A trader can find himself filthy rich one minute and upside down the next.

Let's say you buy one contract of 1000-ounce silver (i.e., you are "long" a CBOT *mini*-silver contract) at $32 an ounce. The market value of the contract is then $32,000. If the margin requirement is 20 percent, you would have to put up $6,400 to hold the contract overnight. Suppose now that silver prices rise to $38 an ounce. A $6 an ounce profit on 1000 ounces is $6,000 — nearly a 100-percent return. Not too shabby.

Naturally, leverage is a double-edged sword. In the zero-sum futures markets, this is especially true — every futures contract has a winning and a corresponding losing side.

If instead of going up to $38 an ounce, the price of silver falls to $26, then the trade's $6 loss would barely leave you enough for cab fare home.

It should also be noted that the futures markets — as opposed to U.S. stock exchange rules — are *marked-to-market*. This means that end-of-day account balances reflect the market price of the contracts held, and deficient accounts must be made good. At $38 an ounce, your account would show a balance of $12,400. On the other hand, at $26 an ounce, your account would show $400 and you would be hit with a *margin call* — meaning, to keep the mini-silver position, you would have to add $6,000 in order to meet the margin requirement. And no: "check's in the mail" won't cut it. Commodity exchange clearing houses insist on a same-day wire transfer or cash.

This is an oversimplification as to how these instruments work, but the point is that before utilizing options or futures for precious metals ownership take the time necessary to understand all the intricacies involved. Most active traders tend to spend the better part of their day keeping track of their positions. So before taking this step, make sure you have the right temperment and the right tools for the lightning-quick environment of futures trading. Overpaying for a rare coin is one thing, but a mistake in the futures markets can turn into a monumental disaster in a heartbeat. If you are in any way unsophisticated or inexperienced with exchange-traded vehicles, the commodity futures and options markets are probably not the best places to learn.

One final note of caution: There are certain off-exchange companies that offer leveraged contracts. Their sales pitches can be quite enticing, but don't be fooled — the commissions on these products are very high. It is tough enough to successfully speculate on short-term swings in the market with low commissions, but it is nearly impossible to beat the market when you need a big move in your direction just to reach the trade's break-even point.

An **Individual Retirement Account** is another way to own physical metals without having physical possession of them. Metals purchased in this way must be held by a third party vaulting facility, but they are owned by one's IRA account and are segregated in the vault with that designation. Federal law limits what forms of gold and silver can be held by these accounts, and one needs the cooperation of a rare coin or bullion dealer, an IRA administrator that specializes in non-traditional IRA accounts and a certified vaulting facility. While the costs are not great, typically about $150 a year for the IRA administrator and about the same for annual storage, precious metals IRAs may not be cost effective for less than $30,000 because of those fees.

For amounts larger than $30,000, not only are the fees reasonable, but, at least as of now, it is possible to take distributions of the actual metal. Rules are always changing when it comes to retirement accounts, especially considering the numerous changes to the tax code starting in 2013, so it is recommended to research all current rules and regulations that apply and consult a tax accountant before participating in the precious metals markets in this way.

Furthermore, because the metals must be purchased by a third party coin or bullion dealer who sends the metals to the vaulting facility (so that the actual silver or gold never touches the hands of the IRA owner), it is important to research prices charged for the metal. Sometimes the spreads on these purchases can be unusually high.

Let's say that you buy 2008 proof gold eagles for your IRA account. Those actual coins will be sent by the dealer to the vaulting facility, and the vaulting facility will hold those exact coins for you, the IRA owner. Should 2008 proof eagles ever become numismatic items, selling above their gold value, then you would directly benefit because your IRA owns those specific coins.

Physical Possession

When it comes to the buying and selling of rare coins and precious metals not only is one usually involved directly in the transaction but also personally and physically responsible for the safe storage, maintenance and transfer of the items involved.

There are a variety of methods for buying and selling precious metals and coins in which physical possession is involved. Because the actual items must pass from one person to another, almost all of these methods involve a transaction of value for value. Cash on the barrelhead, as it were. But coins, gold and silver are not only bought and sold for cash, check and other dollar instruments — lest we forget, gold, silver and coins are the original money, and any kind of exchange or barter to which two parties can agree is acceptable.

The physical trading market is extremely diverse. There are many buyers and sellers, some of whom will pay or ask different prices than other buyers and sellers for similar coins and precious metals. While physical trading takes place online or through large brokerages, a great number of trades occur between individuals and other individuals, or between individuals and a wide range of dealers who specialize in physical transactions.

Each trade is a separate transaction and is usually private and not recorded or published. There are no central exchanges through which these trades are made. Markets where the actual physical materials are exchanged are not centralized or controlled in the same way as stocks, bonds and other traditional investment areas. Frequently receipts and bills of sale are exchanged, especially when professional dealers are involved. But in many cases, especially trades between private individuals, no records of the transactions are kept whatsoever. The trading of rare coins and physical precious metals are two of the relatively few money-related arenas where buying, selling and bartering can remain completely private.

Dawson City, at the confluence of the Klondike and Yukon Rivers in Canada, was the center of the Klondike Gold Rush at the turn of the 20th century. With the recent spike in gold prices, Alaska and the northwest region of Canada have seen a resurgence of prospectors with the same hopes, dreams and hardships as the men in this photograph.

Buying, selling and trading rare coins and precious metals with people you know personally is an effective way to execute transactions. Coin collectors who get to know each other do this all the time, as one might have an extra example of a particular coin desired by the other. Without any middle men or dealer involvement, the seller tends to get a little more and the buyer tends to pay a little less than they otherwise would. A good deal for both parties.

Cultivating these relationships, in addition to the comraderie of a shared interest, can be especially useful in a pinch, when there is some urgency to making a transaction. You may be the beneficiary of a cash-strapped friend who accepts your low-bid offer on a coin you've been hoping to acquire. Or, conversely, you may be the one who needs cash in a hurry, and it's your trading partner who comes to your rescue.

The obvious problem is that with so many different types of coins, it is improbable that you will personally know someone who has exactly you're looking for.

An extension of the aforementioned handshake method is using local want ads or craigslist.org. But beware — it's one thing to sell a couch or some low-value item on Craigslist and quite another to advertise that you are in possession of valuables that are extremely difficult to trace when stolen.

While want ads can be an expedient medium of exchange, they carry the risk of face-to-face business with people you don't know. Buyers may tender ridiculously low offers, be a robbery threat or, worse, a physical threat. Always take reasonable precautions when working with someone in this way. Instead of meeting a stranger in your home at night, it is probably prudent to meet them at a crowded diner in broad daylight.

Falling loosely into this category are garage and estate sales. These can sometimes yield good deals. Coins sold at garage sales tend to be lower end, but you never know. Occasionally there may be someone selling granddad's valuable collection at bargain-basement prices. For collectors considering cherrypicking coins in this fashion, it is strongly recommended to have a sharp eye when it comes to grading and pricing raw coins, foremost of which is to know key dates.

An extension of these trading vehicles made possible by technology is online trading. My personal observations and experiences with eBay and similar online services are a mixed bag of good and bad. Sometimes it works well, especially when selling unusual items. On other occasions, it feels like an exercise in frustration and futility.

The main problem with eBay when it comes to selling coins is that it takes a great deal of effort to photograph and list them. These days it is essential to photograph the coins you sell online. A poor quality photo can hurt the sale price or even sabotage the deal altogether. Most dealers who use eBay and other online sales venues hire a computer tech and professional photographer, or have the equipment and expertise to do it in-house. *Numismatic Photography* (Zyrus Press) by Mark Goodman, incidentally, is a good book to learn how to do it yourself. If one is proficient at listing items on eBay and has the time to do it, this can be a good way to sell coins, particularly because it exposes the coins to a large pool of potential buyers.

Buying on eBay — just like selling on eBay — is hit or miss. If one is looking for something strange or unusual, eBay can be a great place to look. There is no question that oftentimes there are excellent buys to be had through eBay and similar services. Doing so, however, frequently depends upon the buyer's knowledge of coins and the seller's lack of knowledge. Dealers have found excellent deals on eBay, but then admitted that it took them a lot of time and energy to find them. Of course, if one likes that sort of thing, or if a buyer's time is so limited they can only shop after 10 p.m., buying on eBay might be perfect. There are some collectors and dealers who simply love to buy and sell on eBay, and that is pretty much all they do.

Take note, though, eBay takes a generous percentage for using their services, sometimes as high as 12 percent of the gross sale. And using Paypal for the monetary transaction can cost an additional few percent. Another disadvantage of eBay is that one must also handle the packaging and shipping. It is not uncommon for customers to return an item claiming it was improperly graded or described. Sometimes these items are returned damaged or even replaced.

While most online sellers are sincere private individuals and legitimate dealers, rip-off artists do exist. These con men seem to operate out of China and the same countries that perpetrate various email scams — but they are by no means limited to foreign nationals. Sometimes the clever buggers even put their counterfeit coins into counterfeit PCGS holders. For a list of commonly counterfeited coins, visit the PCGS website (www.pcgs.com).

Regardless of the aforementioned, eBay has become an important force in the numismatic world as prices realized on coins in eBay auctions are commonly listed with the results of other numismatic auctions.

Another notable online buying source is Collectors Corner (www.collectorscorner.com), a division of the Certified Coin Exchange. The site is geared more toward collectors than investors. Coins listed for sale are presented in a catalog style as opposed to the eBay auction format. Usually — but not always — there are high-quality photos of the coins. The thing to be aware of is that dealers frequently offer their hard-to-get-rid-of coins — which basically means it has the drawbacks of any online catalog. The big advantage of Collectors Corner is that all the sellers are member professional coin dealers. Thus, one avoids the drawbacks of eBay when it comes to providing a platform for scam dealers, counterfeiters and other flimfammers. Also, the fees for member dealers are quite low, which theoretically ought to lower their asking prices.

Rare Coin Dealers

Regardless of other trading sources, at some point there is a fair likelihood a purchaser will require the services of a professional dealer. This is true for both rare coins and precious metals.

While the basic functions that dealers provide are uniform, the business models between them are widely divergent. Some conduct their business online, and some run neighborhood coin shops. Some specialize in ancient coins, and some in bullion. There are large corporations that market products on television, vest-pocket dealers who travel the trade show circuit, and everything in between.

Dealers facilitate buying and selling by having the liquidity to quickly purchase coins and having a wide variety of coins available for sale. Most dealers both buy and sell, but some emphasize one or the other.

When choosing a dealer it is important to consider their business model. Obviously your interests should align. There's no sense talking to a U.S. modern coin specialist if you're looking for a 1656 Cromwell Halfcrown.

Take the time to talk with the individual who would be handling your purchase or sale. Make sure you feel comfortable with his advice. Do not hesitate to ask any questions you may have. A good rule of thumb in this regard is the only "stupid" question is the one you didn't ask. Someone who dodges or refuses to give straight answers, or who pushes too strongly in a disagreeable direction might not be the person to do business with.

Buying and selling coins is almost always a trade-off between time and money. If you have the time and expertise to hunt for the coins you wish to purchase and have the contacts and other reliable venues in which to sell, you probably don't need the regular services of a professional dealer. But for most people, the additional costs of using a professional dealer is money well spent. It's almost never a bad idea to have a second set of expert eyes on your financial matters, and this is especially true when it comes to numismatics.

For bullion buyers, transactions are more straightforward: The look and quality of bullion coins or bars is less important. There are plenty of reputable online sources. And, if leary of internet transactions, chances are good there is a nearby coin shop that actively trades gold and silver bullion. The important criteria with bullion is to buy and sell at competitive prices. As long as the spread between the spot price and your cost is within industry standards or better, it makes little difference whether you buy, say, Johnson Matthey or Engelhard silver bars.

Coin Shops

Coin shops are perhaps the oldest type of venue for buying and selling coins. Traditionally, coin shops also deal in other collectibles, especially in related fields such as stamps, watches, diamonds, jewelry and precious metals. Most will have extended areas of interest, which could include items as diverse as Disney dollars or casino chips.

Brick and mortar establishments tend to focus on serving the local community. Some will sponsor coin clubs, or have events where their customers can buy and sell, kind of like a mini coin show, and most are owner operated.

These buy-and-sell shops cater to collectors and are frequently a good venue for selling your coins as well as buying them. The disadvantage is that many of the coins held in inventory tend to be lower-end collectible material — which is fine if you collect low-end coins. On the other hand, if you have the financial ability and the desire to work with more expensive and exotic coins, it is probable that you'll have to expand your hunting grounds beyond your favorite local coin shop.

Most coin shops prefer to develop a long-term relationship with their customers. However, just as in any industry, there are some bad apples; some coin shop owners are more interested in "ripping a deal" than cultivating lasting business opportunities. Since there are no price controls on rare coins or physical precious metals, it is up to you, the customer, to gain sufficient knowledge to know the difference between a reputable coin dealer and a fly-by-night gold scrap-buying operation.

Coin Shows

Coin shows are just like coin shops, except that instead of a single brick and mortar establishment for one business, a coin show gathers anywhere from a handful to hundreds of dealers of all kinds in one place at the same time. There are shows in every state and most major cities. Lists of coin shows can be found online and in numismatic periodicals.

The proximity of so many dealers in one place creates a terrific infrastructure for trading. There is an obvious advantage to being able to examine and compare coins in person before buying as well as to obtain offers from different dealers before selling.

Disadvantages of coin shows are that they can be time consuming and, if far away, attending can be expensive. Most coin shows are quite small — less than 30 dealers — and therefore the specific coins of interest may not be present or available. Meanwhile, the major coin shows are exhaustingly large, with hundreds of dealers exhibiting. First time visitors to these large coin shows usually leave overwhelmed and worn out, much like first time visitors to the Louvre. But the more times you attend the major shows, the more you will develop a systematic way in which to economize your time and effort.

Most transactions at coin shows are done in cash, or some combination of cash and trade, unless the parties have a previously established business relationship. Big dollar transactions are sometimes made through bank transfers, with the exchange taking place once the seller receives confirmation. But, as coin shows often run through the weekend when retail banking operations are closed, even big dollar transactions are usually cash and carry.

Lawrence D. Goldberg sets up at the San Francisco coin show, April 2010.

There is no infrastructure to enable a dealer to accept a check from an unknown buyer with the certainty his check will clear. Furthermore, most dealers do not accept credit cards for large purchases or for bullion in which the spreads are so tight the bank charges alone would eat up all their profit margin. This is changing somewhat — technology has made it cost effective for dealers to accept credit cards for certain types of purchases. Smart phones now have apps that are also making money transactions easier.

And, in many cases, coin shows simply provide the venue where people lay the groundwork for transactions that will take place at a later date.

Coin shows are excellent venues for selling, too. A seller has the opportunity to show his coins to several dealers to see who will make the best offer. Generally speaking, the seller gets an immediate payment by cash, or a check from known dealers. Coin shows are also a great place to learn: In addition to picking the brains of professional dealers, there are frequently terrific seminars dealing with specific aspects of numismatics. Often there are also displays of unusually rare, museum quality coins and other numismatic-related materials.

Coin shows also provide the opportunity to establish a rapport with a few dealers before offering a large accumulation for sale. First, it is physically demanding to roll around a large, heavy suitcase full of coins. Second, while security inside a coin show is invariably excellent, a heavy suitcase paints a target for crooks outside the venue. A preferred method is to take only a few coins to the show as samples — and in lieu of your whole collection to bring instead an inventory list — and to use the venue as a means to accomplish the following two things:

- Find the dealers with whom you feel most comfortable and, of those, which ones are interested in purchasing your coins
- Determine price ranges and expectations for the coins you wish to sell

Though the smaller coin shows may only go for a day, the bigger ones run for two or three days, with the really big ones, like those sponsored by the American Numismatic Association, for as many as five days. So, many collectors will attend the first day with finding the right dealer(s) as their only objective, and then return on the second and third days to conclude a sale, or to arrange a later time and place to meet.

Auctions

The auction business has expanded in recent years. An increasing volume of auction activity now takes place over the internet through venues like Heritage Auctions, Teletrade, Great Collections, CCE/Collectors Corner and eBay, touched upon earlier in this chapter — but it is worth revisiting here because auctions are significant apart from those aspects involving the internet.

Auctions are an important part of the rare coin business. Since sale prices are public knowledge, as opposed to undisclosed private sales typical to the rare coin business, auction prices are often used as a benchmark upon which future sales prices are based.

As with art auctions, coin auctions are particularly effective when dealing with famous collections and super rare, expensive or unusual coins of which there are many high-end buyers. This traditional type of auction is usually held in conjunction with one of the major coin shows.

Some dealers have reported that they no longer attend auctions because the "non-professional" buyers push prices so high that they cannot buy at a level low enough to resell at a profit.

While that may make it seem as though selling at auction is the best way to sell coins, such a conclusion is not warranted. Many coins do not sell well at auction, and many do not sell at all because their reserve price is too high. The point here is that auction prices are often executed further out on the bell curve as compared to, say, a coin show. Where there is a greater chance of snapping up a great deal, there is also a greater chance of getting burned.

Some auctions are very well attended, and others are not. Since it is necessary to submit coins for auctions well in advance (so the auctioneers can prepare the catalogue and match the number of lots with their time limitations), committing to an auction could eliminate other selling opportunities.

Auction houses, it should be known, charge upwards of 15 percent to the buyer on top of the hammer price, and may even charge an extra few percent to the seller if the total value of the collection consigned is below some arbitrary standard they've set.

Buying by auction is tricky and not for the faint of heart. At major auctions you will be competing against highly experienced collectors and professional dealers. You'll have to be comfortable making snap decisions, potentially involving tens of thousands of dollars. While auctions can no doubt be very exciting, it can also be intimidating to the uninitiated. For this reason, many well-heeled collectors use dealers to represent them when they want to buy at auction, and will consult dealers when it comes to choosing which auction to use for selling their important coins.

It is highly recommended to attend at least a couple of auctions as an observer before jumping into the fray and bidding on coins.

A Final Word of Caution

When dealing with precious metals and coins, as with any business opportunity, it is wise to be mindful of the old adage: *If it sounds too good to be true, it probably is.*

Some of the companies that wish to purchase your gold, silver and rare coins — or sell them to you — employ deceptive marketing practices. Their advertising and sales pitches — all dolled up with slick TV and print ads, celebrity pitchmen, fancy color brochures, DVDs, perhaps even a free coin — create the smoke in which they obscure high commission costs. They count on the psychology of *better the devil you know.*

For the most part, these companies deliver quality products. Their bullion coins are real, their numismatic coins are certified by PCGS or NGC, and their customer service reps and sales staff — if not particularly knowledgeable — are exceptionally friendly.

One particular marketing ploy — admirable if only for its sheer deviousness — is offering to buyback coins at prices above the market. Never mind your original purchase price was grossly inflated! Now you're locked into dealing with this company and their artificial market and outrageous bid-ask spreads.

The bottom line is their million-dollar advertising budget has to be accounted for one way or another. Typically, it is accomplished by passing the additional costs to their customers through higher prices.

All of this goes double for television shopping networks. Although, I suppose, if you were in a pinch to get a niece or a nephew a quick birthday gift, an overpriced Statehood quarters coin collection is better than a late Hallmark card.

Pawn shops are possibly the worst place to sell your coins. The whole business model of a pawn shop is to buy at a tiny fraction of an item's value. Furthermore, most pawn shop proprietors are not coin experts. They do not have the contacts to quickly buy and sell at market value prices, and therefore will tend to underestimate the value of any given coin. Thus, pawnbrokers pay far less on average than professional dealers. Unless you are in a life-or-death situation and in desperate need of cash do not sell your numismatic coins here.

On the other hand, it is possible that pawn shops will yield a good buy from time to time. Not being experts in the field, there is a chance a coin's true value will be missed. Several people have told me about the excellent purchases they made at pawn shops. All of those circumstances, however, involved lower-end coins.

That said, of the numerous times I have been inside a pawn shop, never once did I see any big bargain — so it isn't something I make of habit of doing.

Note that some coins shops also have pawn licenses, which enables them to purchase jewelry and other valuable items. These should not be confused with regular pawns shops.

Chapter Three

Gold and Silver: Which is Better and How Best to Own Them

ONE OF THE QUESTIONS FREQUENTLY ASKED with regard to bullion is whether it is better to buy gold or silver. That's like asking whether it is better to eat a hot dog or a hamburger. As gold and silver are the most popular hedges against inflation of the currency, they both accomplish the same economic purpose. While at times the price of one might rise while the other drops, or rise and fall in different percentages on any given day, over the long term, gold and silver tend to rise and fall together and react to economic news in similar ways.

For most people, therefore, the choice between gold and silver usually revolves around one's specific needs, rather than a particular market advantage of one metal over the other.

In examining this issue, it is useful to look at the ratio of value between gold and silver. Looking at U.S. numismatic history, where a one-ounce gold coin was worth $20 and a one-ounce silver coin was worth $1, it is clear that for years the de facto ratio of gold to silver was 20:1. Later, when gold was fixed at $35 per ounce, while silver prices still hovered around $1 per ounce, the ratio went to 35:1.

In 1989, with gold at around $400 per ounce and silver at around $5.50 per ounce, the ratio was around 72:1. Today, assuming gold at $1500 per ounce and silver at $27 per ounce, the ratio is about 55:1. Some of the more aggressive predictions of future gold and silver prices suggest $5000 per ounce for gold and $100 per ounce for silver. If that occurs, the ratio would be 50:1.

The long-term trend, going back more than a 100 years, reveals gold outperforming silver. Even so, there have been times when the ratio of gold to silver went as high as 100:1 and below 20:1, so obviously these ratios can fluctuate significantly in the short and long term due to a variety of market and economic factors. There is no guarantee or even a particular reason that an increasing gold/silver ratio should continue.

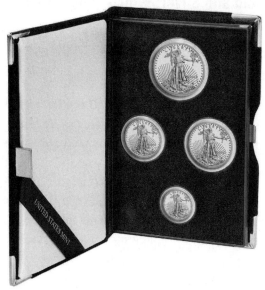

U.S. Mint Gold Eagle proof set includes one-ounce, half-ounce, quarter-ounce and tenth-ounce coins. The 2013 collection retails for $3,260.

There has been a great deal of news speculation, not all of it from reliable sources, that silver will strongly outperform gold in the coming years. While at times during the last few years it seemed as if silver had increased more percentage-wise than gold, the ratio as of August 2013 is not much different than it was in 1999.

The most frequently cited — and probably most convincing — reason is that silver is used industrially, and that in many of its industrial processes and applications, silver is consumed and destroyed, which reduces the supply of silver. The more that supply is reduced, the higher the price of silver will go because its important industrial uses cannot be achieved by other metals. The industrial demand for silver is also impacted by the strength of the economy: A stronger economy will almost certainly increase the demand for silver.

Another frequently cited reason is that so much silver has been mined already that even the unexploited supply not yet mined is extremely low. How one can reliably measure how much silver remains undiscovered is questionable, and the silver mining volume has been fairly consistent over the last decade. So while this could be true, as of now there is not sufficient evidence to be conclusive.

A third reason is that in the event of a financial collapse, people who cannot afford quantities of gold — which is most people — will need to use silver for ordinary purchases, and therefore the demand for silver will correspondingly increase, driving up the price.

These are the three most commonly mentioned reasons that silver would outperform gold. If one explores the internet, one will find extreme estimates as to the amount of silver that has been destroyed. Some claim that silver will soon be less common than gold. Considering how much silver already exists in the form of coinage, sterling silverware and jewelry, and given its yearly production figures, this assertion is borderline ridiculous.

If one spends any significant time researching, one will come across outlandish claims, not only for silver but also for platinum, palladium and other precious metals. This is nothing new. The commodity markets are notorious for reacting to rumors and conjecture, and therefore it is no surprise that farfetched predictions and hype make up part of the avalanche of available "information." In some cases, it is the work of over enthusiastic conspiracy theorists, and in others it might be the work of marketers who stand to profit from promoting an extreme position. The moral of this story is don't believe everything you read. When researching the markets, it is a good idea to consider the source and to evaluate the material with a healthy dose of skepticism.

None of these factors or issues mentioned above, whether taken singly or together, comprise a sufficiently convincing case that silver will increase at a greater percentage rate than gold. It is impossible to forecast which factors will be dominant in the future. Common sense dictates not to have all your eggs in one basket. With that in mind, it is recommended to have both gold and silver in your portfolio. That way, no matter what unexpected event occurs, or which metal performs better, you'll be covered.

Regardless of the precise makeup of precious metals in your portfolio, knowing the advantages and disadvantages of gold and silver is helpful in choosing what will best serve your specific needs.

The main advantages of gold are:
- It allows for a great deal of value to be put in a small space
- It is easily portable
- It comes in a wide variety of denominations
- Its value is easily recognized
- It is rapidly and easily traded or sold
- It is durable
- It is the world standard of stored value

The main disadvantages of gold are:
- Since it is easily portable, it is a more attractive target for theft
- Stolen gold is difficult to trace
- Purity and quantity per unit of gold is not always uniform, which sometimes causes confusion

Silver shares the main advantages and disadvantages of gold with the following exceptions:
- It takes much more weight and volume of silver to match the monetary value of gold, which makes it more difficult to move and store
- It comes in low value denominations
- It is the secondary world standard of stored value
- It has industrial applications that can cause it to fluctuate with industrial as well as monetary issues

The fact that gold comprises much greater value per ounce than silver can be hugely consequential when working with larger quantities. Let's say you wish to transport $100,000 in hard assets. With gold at $1,600 an ounce, the amount would be 62.5 ounces — just over five pounds (12 troy ounces equals one pound) — which would take up little more than six cubic inches and easily fit into a purse, backpack or computer case.

On the other hand, at $30 an ounce, about 3300 ounces of silver would be necessary to equal $100,000, and it would weigh close to 300 pounds.

Silver is almost half as heavy as gold. An ounce of gold is .098 of a cubic inch, while an ounce of silver is .16 of a cubic inch and therefore takes up almost twice as much room per ounce as does gold. So, while silver is portable, it is not nearly as convenient to transport when it comes to large amounts.

Bullion

When we speak of bullion, we are almost always refering to gold, silver, platinum or palladium — as opposed to industrial or base metals like copper and aluminum. The word bullion connotes that its metal content alone determines its value. Usually, bullion is made in precise increments of weight, such as grams or ounces. One distinguishing feature of bullion is that it is easy to calculate and track its value. In other words, its value fluctuates precisely with the market value of the underlying precious metal.

To be regarded as bullion, the purity of the gold or silver is an important factor. Bullion usually refers to bars or coins that are pure or mostly pure. There are some exceptions. A gold Krugerand, for instance, is 10 percent copper — an alloy added for strength. However, a Krugerand still contains a full ounce of pure gold. It weighs roughly 1.1 ounces, but the value is based on its precious-metal content, which is the one ounce of gold.

If you have an ounce of gold — be it a Krugerand, Maple Leaf, Eagle or bar — and want to know its value, all you have to do is check the price of gold that day, which is posted online at major dealers like Kitco (www.kitco.com) and other brokerages, or printed in the business section of daily newspapers. The same holds true for silver.

The Mobius-ring pendant contains precisely one ounce of 24K gold. *Photo courtesy Charles Sherman*

Knowing the purity of the metal is critical because precious metals come in a wide variety of forms, including bars, coins, gold flakes, jewelry, ingots, nuggets, even dental fillings — all of which have different levels of purity. The melt value of 14K gold is worth 55 percent of the melt value of 24K or pure gold. Knowing and being able to easily show the purity of gold is important when it comes to selling, bartering or trading bullion. It is for this reason that most bullion buyers prefer bars from highly respected and recognized manufacturers, or coins made by governments known for their accuracy in the metal content. It is also why people who accumulate scrap gold or silver usually refine it to the pure metal, which makes it much easier to value when trading.

Some people prefer jewelry, because they enjoy wearing it. Yet, jewelry is difficult to assay (prove the purity) unless it is hallmarked. Even then, it is much harder to sell except to dealers or jewelers who will charge a substantial discount to retail for their trouble. If one wishes to trade gold jewelry, it will be necessary to invest in a digital scale, and a gold and silver testing kit — which is messy, highly acidic and a real pain to work with.

Not long ago, I had a discussion with a friend of mine, sculptor and jewelry designer Charles Sherman, about creating jewelry that contains a specific amount of gold, say an ounce, half ounce or quarter ounce.

Inspired by this discussion, he took one of his more prolific motifs, a Mobius ring, and designed a one-ounce pendant of pure 24K gold.

He informs me that other designs with exact precious metals quantities are on the way. Whether or not this becomes a trend or style remains to be seen.

Modern Gold Coins Minted by Governments

While other countries besides those listed below also make gold coins, the following are the most commonly desired one-ounce gold bullion coins. These coins are recognized by everyone and boast high-quality manufacture and consistent purity. For this reason, they will trade at a (quasi-fixed) premium to spot prices.

- American Gold Eagles
- Canadian Gold Maple Leafs
- South African Gold Krugerands
- Chinese Pandas
- Australian Gold Nuggets
- Austrian Gold Philharmonics

Premium gold bullion coins can also be purchased in smaller than one-ounce denominations, typically half ounce, quarter ounce, tenth ounce and occasionally twentith ounce. Spreads are larger on smaller denominations, sometimes running as high as 15 percent or more — so unless there is a specific need for smaller denominations of gold, I generally advise against them.

With the passage of the Coinage Act of 1873, production of Seated Liberty dollars stopped. The minting of silver dollars would resume in 1878 after the passage of the Bland-Allison Act with the Morgan dollar.

The following is a list of foreign gold coins and how much of an ounce of gold they contain. This is essential information for anyone who desires to own foreign-made gold coins that do not contain exactly one ounce of gold.

It is interesting to note how few world gold coins are in a standard increment of an ounce, or even in grams, the metric unit of weight. Naturally, this can be very confusing to people who are new to the market. In the World Gold Coins table on pages 81 to 83, purity is omitted so only the actual amount of pure gold in each coin, measured in ounces, is noted.

Some rare coin and bullion dealers, including some larger firms that advertise nationally on popular radio and television shows, specialize in selling these coins. They frequently charge premiums of 20 to 30 percent above bullion value. In some cases, these foreign bullion gold coins have been certified by PCGS or NGC and the selling company will call them "numismatic." Be that as it may, when you go to sell, their actual value is only the gold. Therefore, be vigilant when buying foreign gold and double check the math so that you know exactly how much actual gold weight you are receiving.

WORLD GOLD COINS: ACTUAL GOLD WEIGHTS				
Country	Coin	Date Range	Variety	AGW
Argentina	Un Argentino	1881-1896		.2334
Austria	1 Ducat	1915		.1106
Austria	4 Ducat	1915		.4430
Austria	4 Florin/10 Francs	1870-1892		.0933
Austria	8 Florin/20 Francs	1870-1892		.1867
Austria	10 Corona	1892-1912		.0980
Austria	20 Corona	1892-1912		.1960
Austria	100 Corona	1915		.9802
Belgium	20 Frank	1867-1914		.1867
Brazil	20,000 Reis	1850		.5286
Canada	5 Dollars	1912-1914		.2419
Canada	10 Dollars	1912-1914		.4834
Canada	100 Dollars	1976	Beaded Borders	.2500
Canada	100 Dollars	1976	Plain Border	.5000
Canada	100 Dollars	1987-1999		.2500
Chile	100 Pesos	1926-1980	aka Diez Condores	.5886
Columbia	5 Peso	1924-1930		.2355
Cuba	2 Peso	1915-1916		.0483
Cuba	4 Peso	1915-1916		.1935
Cuba	5 Peso	1915-1916		.2419
Cuba	10 Peso	1915-1916		.4838
Cuba	20 Peso	1915-1916		.9676
Denmark	10 Kroner	1873-1917		.1296
Denmark	20 Kroner	1915-1917		.2592
France	5 Francs	1854-1869		.0467
France	10 Francs	1850-1914		.0933
France	20 Francs	1806-1914	Kings/Angels/Roosters	.1867
France	40 Francs			.3734
France	50 Francs			.4667

WORLD GOLD COINS: ACTUAL GOLD WEIGHTS

Country	Coin	Date Range	Variety	AGW
France	100 Francs			.9335
France	100 Francs	1986	St. of Lib. (Gold)	.5028
France	100 Francs	1986	St. of Lib. (Platinum)	.6430
Germany	10 Marks			.1152
Germany	20 Marks			.2304
Great Britain	½ Sovereign	1817-Date	King/Queen	.1177
Great Britain	Sovereign	1817-Date	King/Queen	.2354
Hungary	4 Forint/10 Francs	1870-1891		.0934
Hungary	8 Forint/20 Francs	1870-1892		.1867
Hungary	10 Korona	1892-1915		.0980
Hungary	20 Korona	1892-1916		.1960
Hungary	100 Korona	1907-1908	Restrike	.9802
Italy	20 Lire	1861-1897		.1867
Mexico	1 Peso Gold	1888-1890		.0476
Mexico	2 Peso Gold	1919-1947		.0482
Mexico	2.5 Peso Gold	1918-1947		.0602
Mexico	5 Peso Gold	1905-1955		.1205
Mexico	10 Peso Gold	1905-1959		.2411
Mexico	20 Peso Gold	1917-1959		.4823
Mexico	50 Peso Gold	1921-1947		1.2057
Netherlands	10 Guilders	1875-1933	King or Queen	.1947
Norway	20 Kroner	1874-1910		.2593
Panama	100 Balboa	1975-1984		.2361
Peru	1/5 Libra (Pound)	1906-1969		.2411
Peru	½ Libra (Pound)	1902-1969		.1177
Peru	Libra (Pound)	1898-1969		.2354
Peru	100 Soles	1950-1970		1.3544
Poland	10 Zlotych	ND (1925)(w)	Boleslaw 1	.0933
Poland	20 Zlotych	ND (1925)(w)	Boleslaw 1	.1867

WORLD GOLD COINS: ACTUAL GOLD WEIGHTS				
Country	**Coin**	**Date Range**	**Variety**	**AGW**
Russia	5 Rouble, Gold	1897-1911		.1244
Russia	7.5 Rouble, Gold	1897		.1867
Russia	10 Rouble, Gold	1898-1911		.2489
Russia	15 Rouble, Gold	1897		.3734
South Africa	1 Rand	1961-1983		.1177
South Africa	2 Rand	1961-1983		.2354
Sweden	20 Kroner	1873-1900		.2593
Switzerland	10 Francs, Gold	1883-1922		.0933
Switzerland	20 Francs, Gold	1883-1947		.1867
Turkey	50 Kurush	1923		.0517
Turkey	500 Kurush	1942-1980		1.0338
USA	Type 1 G$1	1849-1854	Type 1	.0484
USA	Type 2 G$1	1854-1856	Type 2	.0484
USA	Type 3 G$1	1856-1889	Type 3	.0484
USA	2.5 Dollars	1840-1929		.1209
USA	3 Dollars	1854-1889		.1451
USA	5 Dollars	1839-1929		.2419
USA	10 Dollars	1838-1933		.4837
USA	20 Dollars	1849-1933		.9675
Uruguay	5 Pesos	1930		.2501

Medallion or "Art" Gold

U.S. medallions are one-ounce and half-ounce gold coins featuring the portraits of famous Americans. Some of the more notable ones include Grant Wood, Marian Anderson, Mark Twain, Willa Cather, Louis Armstrong, Frank Lloyd Wright, Robert Frost, Alexander Calder, Helen Hayes and John Steinbeck.

Medallions are not considered collectible per se, so don't let someone con you into believing that because there is a limited amount of a particular design that they will someday be prized collectibles. They are not particularly beautiful, but they are well manufactured and have a consistent purity. They are gold, but are considered in the trade as *junk* gold. As a result, they usually are discounted below the gold price, but only by a few percent. Most dealers simply melt them.

There are other kinds of gold coins, but those mentioned above are the main ones. It is advisable to stick with the mainstream when it comes to gold bullion. Mainstream coins are easier to buy, easier to sell, and enjoy the lowest spreads.

Silver Bullion

Most countries that mint one-ounce gold coins also mint one-ounce silver bullion coins. One ounce has long been the preferred measure of silver, and that remains true today. It is one of the best ways to own silver. Some of the most popular one-ounce silver coins are:

- American Silver Eagles
- Chinese Silver Pandas
- Canadian Silver Maple Leafs
- Australian Timber Wolves
- Mexican Libertads

There are other one-ounce silver coins not made by governments but by privately-owned entities as diverse as mining companies and charitable organizations. There are far too many to mention, although Sunshine Mines is one of the more popular. These are commonly called *silver rounds*. Often they promote liberty, the Constitution, or any variety of religious — usually Christian — themes. Silver rounds are actively traded and since they contain one ounce of .999 pure silver, they are easily bought and sold at or near the silver spot price.

Platinum and Palladium

As with gold and silver bullion, countries such as the United States, Russia, China and Australia mint platinum and/or palladium coins. While they certainly carry value and move with the underlying precious metal, these coins are less commonly traded and far fewer people buy and sell them as compared to gold and silver.

There are stories about people who have confused platinum for silver — easy for a novice to do as the two metals look remarkably similar. For these reasons, they are not as practical as gold or silver for the average person. However, if one desires to diversify with platinum and palladium coins, they are easily available.

Gold and Silver Bars

Gold and silver bars are made by a wide variety of private manufacturers, are commonly traded and usually offer the narrowest spreads of all forms of bullion. The ease of buying and selling bars largely depends on how much silver or gold they contain, and also, whose *hallmark* is on the bar.

Major hallmarks like Credit Suisse, Johnson Mathey and Engelhard are readily recognized and accepted by dealers. Oddball brands might have to be re-assayed if the dealer has any doubt whatsoever that it is pure silver or gold. This is a cumbersome and expensive process, perhaps costing 10 percent of the bar's value, which again shows the prudence of sticking with major hallmarks. Frequently, dealers will buy minor brands without re-assay, but pay less per ounce. Silver and gold bars exhibiting unusual or historic hallmarks are highly collectible and often fetch hefty premiums above the value of their silver or gold content.

Recently, there have been several articles in the numismatic press about counterfeit bars, mainly bars which are gold plated or gold covered bars of tungsten, which has a similar weight to gold. While that concern has subsided somewhat, it is still very possible and is one reason to favor one-ounce gold coins over bars.

The size of the bars can affect the ease at which they can be sold. One-ounce silver bars and one-ounce gold bars are fairly easy to negotiate. Ten-ounce and 100-ounce silver bars are also fairly easy to buy and sell, despite the fact that a 100-ounce silver bar weighs around eight pounds and is worth more than $2,000 at today's prices. While ten 100-ounce silver bars can be cumbersome, they are not nearly as difficult to work with as a 1,000-ounce silver bar.

Indeed, 1,000-ounce bars of silver do exist. They are used primarily for professional traders and for backing contracts on the Comex or other trading venues. Their 70-pound weight makes them cumbersome, so while coin dealers buy and sell them from time to time, they are not practical for most people. Of course, there is always someone who wants a 1,000-ounce bar of silver to show off to their friends. If that is you, by all means, let your favorite coin dealer know and I'm sure he'd be delighted to find one for you.

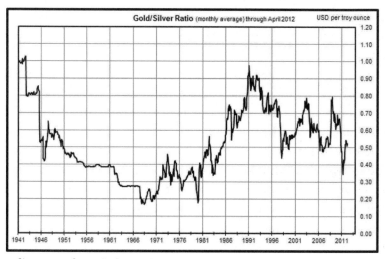

Chart courtesy Commodity Research Bureau

For most people who wish to own 1,000 ounces of silver as a hedge, it is generally much better to have either ten 100-ounce bars, or better still, 1,000 one-ounce coins, preferably in rolls of 20. Smaller denominations simply provide more flexibility if and when one sells — an important benefit.

With gold, it is even more advisable to have one-ounce coins, because of the flexibility they provide when selling. For example, if one has a 10-ounce gold bar, one must find a buyer for the entire bar — at a cost of around $15,000 at today's prices — whereas with 10 one-ounce gold coins, one can either sell all 10 to one person, or one each to 10 different people

Bullion-Related Numismatic Coins

Prior to 1933, the U.S. Government issued gold coins for general circulation in a variety of denominations: $1, $2.50, $3, $5, $10 and $20. All of these are still worth a minimum of their melt value — the amount of gold they contain. If they are well worn or damaged their melt value is probably all they are worth.

However, if in pristine condition they will be worth more than their gold content because they will have numismatic (collector) value. If, in addition to being in pristine condition, they are a rare date, they will have even more and potentially a great deal more numismatic value. Even a coin that is not in pristine condition should be considered a collector coin if it is rare enough. Sometimes, that value can be so far above the value of the gold they contain that they should no longer be considered bullion-related numismatic coins, but strictly as numismatic coins. Two of the highest auction prices ever achieved in numismatic history were for gold coins: the famous Brasher Doubloon and the storied and exceedingly rare 1933 St. Gaudens $20 gold. Each sold for more than $7 million.

Limited production of the first Saint-Gaudens double eagle, a high-relief $20 piece, can fetch more than a half million dollars — Not to be confused with the 2009 edition, which is essentially a 1 oz bullion coin. In Mint State condition, the MMIX ultra high-relief $20 gold coin trades in the neighborhood of $3,000.

For our purposes, bullion-related numismatic gold coins are those which sell for less than double the value of the gold they contain. Because at least 50 percent of the value of these coins is directly determined by their gold content, the value of these coins is primarily, but not exclusively, a reflection of their gold content, and their value fluctuates along with the price of gold. As a general rule, the greater percentage of their value in gold, the more closely they will follow the gold price.

Bullion-related gold coins do not generally include any U.S. coins minted in the $1 and $3 denominations. Unless so severely damaged as to have no numismatic value, these denominations are rare enough that their numismatic value remains well above their bullion value and therefore are considered collectible.

Bullion-related gold coins are easily traded, pretty much the same as are gold bullion coins. Because they are not the exact ounce, half-ounce and quarter-ounce weights, they are somewhat harder to buy and sell. Even so, many people prefer these coins because despite the fact that they buy and sell as bullion, they technically are collectible coins, and are available with dates back into the 1800s, which make them more fun for collectors. They are an excellent way for a collector to enjoy a gold bullion asset, or for an asset-builder who wants a collectible component in his portfolio.

Many people fear the government will someday recall gold like it did in 1933. Since numismatic coins were exempt from that recall, these people believe owning bullion-related U.S. coins gives them a similar exemption in case of such governmental action. Prior to 1933, the entire U.S. monetary system was based on gold and silver. Taking control of the gold was the government's way of responding to a monetary crisis.

Today, gold and silver comprise a much smaller piece of the total economy. Furthermore, because fiat currency has replaced gold and silver as the dominant vehicle of trade, gold and silver have a minimal impact on macro-economic issues. For that reason alone, the likelihood of private ownership of gold being outlawed is remote, and it doesn't warrant serious contemplation here.

Bullion-Related Silver Numismatic Coins

Bullion-related silver numismatic coins do not include rare dates and high-grade examples that are strictly collector coins. Like its gold counterpart, bullion-related silver coins derive most or all of their value from their silver content. They come in five basic denominations: nickels, dimes, quarters, half dollars and dollars, and are divided into four basic categories based solely on the percentage of silver they contain, as follows:

- 90-percent silver consists of dimes, quarters and half dollars minted 1964 and earlier and some modern commemorative dollars
- 40-percent silver consists of Kennedy half dollars minted from 1965 to 1970, proof "S" mint Eisenhower dollars, and some commemoratives
- Junk dollars consist of common-date circulated and low-grade uncirculated Morgan and Peace silver dollars
- Silver nickels

90% Silver Bags

The "90%" demarcation can be misleading: Many people believe it implies that for every dollar of face value there is 90 percent of one ounce of silver. It does not. Dimes, quarters and half dollars minted in 1964 and earlier are called 90-percent because their metallic composition is 90-percent silver and 10-percent copper. (Copper is added to increase durability.)

When silver was pegged at one dollar per ounce by the U.S. government, the U.S. Mint would take an ounce of silver and use it to make one dollar's worth of coins. To pay for the minting process, the Mint deducted a portion of the ounce, which is why each dollar in face value of 90-percent U.S. coinage contains .723 ounces of pure silver. It is assumed these circulated coins are significantly worn, so dealers have agreed upon .715 troy ounces per dollar as the standard. True uncirculated original rolls and quantities of common date 90-percent sell for slightly more.

Thus, every $1,000 face value of pre-1965 U.S. silver coins contains 715 ounces of silver and is called a *bag*. This is because originally, when these coins were sent from the mint to banks to be distributed into the economy, they were transported in bags with $1,000 face value. $500 face value of these coins is called a half bag; $250 face value, a quarter bag, and so forth.

These coins are usually traded according to their melt value, in other words, according to the value of silver they actually contain. There is a simple formula that matches face value to silver content.

Let's say you have $1,000 face value of 90-percent silver coins. It could be 2,000 half dollars, 4,000 quarters, 10,000 dimes, or any combination of these so long as the total adds up to $1,000 in face value. To calculate the melt silver content of 90-percent silver, multiply the face value of the coins in dollars by .715.

This gives the silver content measured in ounces. Then, multiply that by the spot price of silver, which is expressed in terms of one ounce. This will give you the *melt value*.

Thus, if the price of silver is $30 an ounce, multiply that times 715 which equals $21,450. Therefore, the melt value of a $1,000 bag of 90-percent silver coins when silver is $30 per ounce is $21,450.

40% Silver

While not the only coins minted by the U.S. government to contain 40-percent silver (some Eisenhower dollars and commemoratives are 40-percent silver), the term "40% silver" generally applies to Kennedy half dollars minted from 1965 to 1970.

Like 90-percent silver, these coins are traded by the bag and their value is calculated according to the face value times the silver melt value. In the case of 40-percent silver, the melt value is about .295, meaning that every $1,000 face value of 40-percent silver contains 295 ounces of pure silver.

To calculate the silver content of 40-percent silver multiply .295 times the price of silver times the face value.

Most dealers charge a significantly larger spread on 40-percent silver coins than they do on 90-percent because there is less demand, and often it takes longer to sell, or must be discounted further to sell rapidly. Also, because they are less pure, a much larger volume and much greater overall coin weight is required to obtain the same silver content as with 90-percent silver or pure silver, making 40-percent silver more cumbersome and difficult to manage.

Some people think this may change in the future. They suggest that since the 60 percent of the coin that is not silver is copper, and copper prices have been going up, that copper values should be added in. Perhaps they are right, or will be right in the future, but at present, it is foolish to pay more for 40-percent silver coins than their silver content alone warrants.

Silver Nickels

Silver nickels are 35-percent silver. Usually called *war nickels*, they were minted from 1943 to 1945 during World War II when nickel was in high demand as a strategic metal. They are easily distinguished not only because their coloring is usually different but because the mintmark is a large letter in the upper half of the coin's reverse. In fact, the "P" nickels are the only U.S. coins made prior to 2000 at the Philadelphia Mint that actually have a "P" on the coin. All other Philadelphia-minted coins do not have a mintmark.

The U.S. Mint placed large mintmarks, including Philadelphia, above Monticello on war nickels so they could easily identified and removed from circulation after WWII. *Image courtesy CCF Numismatics*

Silver nickels are bought and sold by the coin, by the roll, and sometimes by the bag. A roll consists of 40 coins with a face value of $2. The silver content of a war nickel is .0563 of an ounce. Therefore, a roll of war nickels contains 2.252 ounces of silver. At $30 an ounce the total silver melt value of a roll of war nickels is $67.56 or about $1.69 per coin.

The formula for silver nickels is readily available online and other places but is not particularly well known to the general public — many people are completely unaware the United States minted nickels containing silver. For this reason and because silver is only about 35 percent of their total content, war nickels are not in strong demand as bullion coins. As a result, the spread for silver nickels can be exceedingly large particularly when dealing with small quantities.

Silver Dollars

One of the most common forms of bullion-related numismatic coins are Morgan and Peace silver dollars. These coins were minted in huge quantities, often tens of millions per year, which was far more than needed by the economy of the time. Despite the fact that tens of millions were eventually melted down, they still exist in such large quantities that the common dates in circulated condition generally sell at around their melt value or at a small premium.

The value of common date circulated U.S. silver dollars is highly dependent on the price of silver. All Morgan and Peace silver dollars contain .77344 ounces of silver. Thus, melt value of a $1,000 bag of Morgan or Peace silver dollars is 773 ounces. With silver at $30 an ounce, the melt value of a $1,000 bag of silver dollars is $23,190.

Notice that this is slightly above the price for small denomination 90-percent silver coins. Condition, or grade, is also more important for silver dollars than for 90-percent silver: a bag of *culls*, or badly worn and damaged coins, will bring less than a bag of F/VF (fine/very fine) coins, which will bring less than AU (almost uncirculated) grade, which will bring less than uncirculated or BU rolls.

Despite the fact that all silver dollars contain the exact amount of silver, due to collector demand pre-1921 Morgan silver dollars sell at a premium to circulated 1921 Morgan and common date Peace dollars.

For silver bullion purposes, it does not matter what kind of silver dollars one buys, or the condition the coins, provided one pays fair value. All circulated bags of silver dollars will pretty much follow silver prices. BU or uncirculated rolls have more numismatic heft, and can deviate from spot silver prices more readily than circulated ones.

Chapter Four

Grading

THE WAY NUMISMATISTS QUANTIFY the condition of a coin is through *grading*. With very few exceptions, the condition of gold or silver bullion is not important because the main value of these coins is in their bullion content. The only reason one would want to certify a bullion coin is if the marketplace awards a premium to those coins with sufficiently high grades.

The grade of a collectible numismatic coin, on the other hand, is critical to its value. A coin in poor condition might be worth only its face value, whereas a coin of the same denomination, date and mint of origin in superlative condition could be worth many thousands of dollars. It is no surprise then that determining the condition of coins is one of the most controversial aspects of numismatics. While the difference of one grade can make a huge difference in value for some coins, grading differences on other coins might make very little difference.

Mastering the ability to look at a coin and assign it an accurate grade requires great attention to detail, knowledge of grading standards, and a detective-like skill to recognize when coins have been abused or altered. Grading guides like *Photograde* (Zyrus Press) as well as those available at PCGS.com and elsewhere online are helpful, but they are no substitute for practical experience. Knowing about grades — though not necessarily the ability to do it accurately yourself — and how to make sure that the coins you buy are properly graded is absolutely essential for buying numismatic coins.

Business Strikes

Coins are separated into two types of manufacture: business strikes and proof strikes. Business strikes are created to be used as money, and therefore are made less carefully than proof coins, which are made for presentation and collector purposes.

Coins are graded on the Sheldon scale (named after the man who created it) of one to 70, with one being the worst and 70 being the best. Any coin that is graded 60 or better is uncirculated, which means it has no apparent wear but could have bag marks, scratches, dings, toning (naturally occurring oxidation) and other imperfections. A number under 60 indicates at least some wear.

Before the Sheldon numerical scale was adopted by the coin market, the condition of coins was described more generally as cull, fair, about good, good, very good, fine, very fine, extra fine, about uncirculated, uncirculated, choice uncirculated and gem uncirculated.

Naturally, coin dealers and collectors use the Sheldon scale, as it is more precise and is utilized by third-party grading services. Many coin dealers and collectors still use the old coin descriptions, and most use them interchangeably. The old coin descriptions are always used on *raw* coins, which are coins that are not professionally graded and *slabbed* (put into hard plastic cases) by grading services such as PCGS and NGC.

To reduce confusion, third-party grading services use both the old description and the number when stating the grades of coins. For example, if PCGS or NGC grades a coin as a 50 the label will read "AU-50." If it is graded a 55 the label will read "AU-55." If it is graded a 25 the label will read "VF-25." A grade of 60 is uncirculated and graded as Mint State, or MS-60. The informal grade BU refers to any coins with at least an MS-60 grade. A choice condition coin would be described as MS-63, and a gem condition coin would be MS-65.

The grading system enables dealers and collectors to easily describe what they are buying, selling, pricing, or looking to buy. Thus, a client could say he wants a "blast white MS-65 or better 1921 Peace dollar," or a "common date Seated Liberty dollar in AU," or a "1924-D Mercury dime in high gem or MS-67," and a dealer would know exactly the quality of coin desired.

NUMERICAL AND DESCRIPTIVE GRADING RANKS	
N/A	Cull (damaged and/or severely worn)
1-2	Fair, About Good (AG)
3-7	Good (G)
8-11	Very Good (VG)
12-19	Fine (F)
20-39	Very Fine (VF)
40-49	Extra Fine (EF or XF)
50-59	About Uncirculated (AU)
60-61	Uncirculated or Brilliant Uncirculated (Unc or BU)
62-63	Choice Uncirculated (Choice Unc)
64-66	Gem Uncirculated (Gem)
67-69	High Gem
70	Perfect

Proof Strikes

Proof coins are produced with an extra strong strike and special polishing techniques so that they shine with a mirror-like finish.

To denote the condition of a proof coin, the proof designation is combined with the Sheldon scale. Thus, a proof coin in gem condition might have a grade of PF-65, or PR-65, meaning it is a proof coin with a quality 65 on the Sheldon scale of one to 70. A business strike of the same condition would be designated MS-65.

A proof coin that exhibits wear might be designated PF-50, whereas a business strike in similar condition would be designated AU-50. Note that only business strikes use the "old" numismatic names of good, fine, etc. All proof coins use the proof designation, PF or PR, and then the appropriate grade on the Sheldon numerical scale. The abbreviations "PF" and "PR" are used interchangeably, and mean exactly the same thing.

1917 Type 1 obverse Standing Liberty quarter dollar graded MS-64 by PCGS. It received the full-head, or FH, designation as the head of Lady Liberty is fully struck, exhibits a full hairline, and the hole of her ear is visible. *Photo courtesy Lance Keigwin*

Sometimes during the minting process, there might be an excess of die polish when the coin is struck such that the surfaces of the business strike are *mirror like* and resemble the surfaces of a proof. Coins like this are sometimes graded *proof like*, or PL, and if the effect is particularly strong, they are graded *deep mirror proof like,* or DMPL (pronounced "dimple"). This effect is most commonly, but not exclusively, seen with Morgan silver dollars.

If a coin is made as a proof, and is in perfect condition, it would be designated as a PR-70. If its appearance shows a *cameo effect*, a mirror-like surface in the fields, and a satin-like finish on the actual design, or *devices*, it might be graded as a Cameo (e.g., PR-70 Cam) or Deep Mirror Cameo Proof (e.g., PF-70 DCam).

Third-Party Grading

Third-party grading is a relatively new development in the rare coin market. After reading the above paragraphs about grading, it should be apparent why it is attractive to have an objective third party — someone with no vested interest in having the coin grade higher or lower — with the knowledge and expertise to grade valuable coins. Even so, grading rare coins necessarily has an element of subjectivity, and this is the root of every controversy regarding the subject. There are subtle variations in rare coins that individual graders will assign different weights before assigning a final grade, which is why grading is as much an art as it is a science — even today. The significant point of evolution is that the two major grading services, PCGS and NGC, are now far more consistent than when the idea first took shape.

The first significant attempt to provide third-party grading was sponsored by the American Numismatic Association in the early 1980s.

At the time, I was working my first coin industry job at Bowers and Ruddy Galleries in Hollywood, CA, then the largest and most prestigious rare coin company in the world. A couple of the numismatists there were discussing an experiment with the newly announced third-party grading service. They had sent the same coin (I believe it was a Seated Liberty quarter) to the ANA grading service three times. Once it came back as an MS-60, once as an MS-63, and once as an MS-65. Even in 1981, the price difference between an MS-60 and an MS-65 was significant. Everybody had had a good laugh at the ANA's expense.

But the idea would not go away and later in the '80s a multitude of coin dealers started grading services. Their motivation is clear: Third-party grading would be an outstanding marketing tool, particularly for selling coins to new or inexperienced collectors, and especially to investors. Third-party grading answers the first objection an intelligent but unknowledgeable potential buyer asks: "How do I know the coins you are selling are what you say they are?"

Before third-party grading, a coin dealer would have to spend time educating buyers about grading and its significance, or direct them to where they could learn about it. Because of the complexity and the issues surrounding grading, educating neophyte collectors was a time consuming process. Not only did it eliminate the urgency of the sale, it often discouraged the buyer from ever buying rare coins. But with third-party grading, the seller could say: "You don't have to take my word for it, the ANA — a well-respected and impartial grading service — graded this coin and this is what they say it is, not me."

There was a problem with all the early grading services. While they would render an opinion on the grade of a coin, all of their paperwork would have a disclaimer to the effect: *Grading is an art, not a science, and while this is our educated opinion on the grade of this coin, other experts may disagree . . .*

This resulted in disappointed buyers who bought coins they believed were certified at a certain grade, only to find that when they went to sell their coins, dealers would not accept their coins at the same grade at which the individual purchased it. Typically, the grading company had assigned too high a grade, or had *overgraded,* their coins.

Some early grading companies calculated that if they graded coins easy, or liberally, they would get more business from coin dealers who naturally would want their inventory to be as valuable as possible.

Less scrupulous dealers realized they had a great opportunity to buy inexpensive coins, have them overgraded by a certification company, and then sell them to the unsuspecting public at an inflated price, pocketing the difference. This structure had great potential for abuse, especially considering the obvious conflict of interest in cases where dealers formed their own grading companies and graded their own coins.

Additional complications included the very real differences in grading standards, non-uniform methods, lack of oversight and, in some cases, downright fraud. Truly unscrupulous dealers would conspire with equally unscrupulous graders and have polished circulated coins certified as being in gem condition. Many unsuspecting buyers were subjected to significant harm, which in turn caused major credibility issues for legitimate coin dealers.

There was also a serious packaging oversight. Most early grading companies would issue a certificate and sometimes a photo of the coin to show it had been properly certified. Not all of the photos were well done. The coin itself was frequently packaged in a light flexible plastic coin flip, secured only by a staple, which made it possible for coins to be switched out for other coins, or damaged after they were certified.

The method of grading was also an issue. It takes an experienced eye and excellent equipment (lighting, magnifiers, etc.) to judge factors such as luster, marks, wear, placement and severity of scratches that ultimately determine the grade of a coin. Finally, there is the human element. Not even the best grader on the planet is perfect, and even experienced numismatists will sometimes disagree on the grade of a coin. What does one do if two experts disagree on the fair grade for a particular coin?

These are issues that any truly serious grading company would have to overcome.

Delving into the historical details could take a book on its own. The short version is that in December of 1986, the Professional Coin Grading Service was founded. PCGS was determined to grade coins very strictly then enclose each coin individually in a sealed hard plastic case that could only be opened by breaking it — eliminating the possibility of coins being switched out. The certification would remain in force so long as the holder, or slab, was intact.

Coin dealers love to look at coins and have sharp eyes trained through years of experience to

Prototypes not chosen for regular-issue circulation coins are called pattern coins. All patterns have "J" numbers in reference to the author, the late Dr. J. Hewitt Judd, of the subject's definitive book — informally known as the Judd book.

notice every imperfection or feature that might help or hurt the value of a coin. The idea of trusting someone else's eyes was truly revolutionary. Would it work? Would the market accept it?

If PCGS could be successful, it would open up vast markets for rare coins, specifically to new collectors, inexperienced graders, people with poor eyesight or poor grading skills, and those who desired added peace of mind for their purchases.

NGC grading error: The last digit of the date was altered to make it appear like a scare 1804 large cent. It was determined the coin is in fact an 1803 by examing the reverse.

Although the collector had broken it out of its case, the dealer still took the coin back. After learning of its mistake, NGC covered the loss under its guarantee. *Photo courtesy Lance Keigwin*

Toward this end, PCGS not only rendered an opinion about the authenticity and grade of a coin, they guaranteed the authenticity and grade so long as the plastic case into which the coin is sealed remained intact. They backed up that guarantee with a large insurance policy.

A year later, one of the original founders of PCGS set up a competing company that he called the Numismatic Guaranty Corporation, which adopted similar guarantees.

While imperfect, especially at first and sometimes with bizarre results, PCGS and NGC grading did indeed revolutionize the rare coin market. For the first time, buyers of certified coins could be sure that the grade at which they purchased the coin would be honored when they sold. As with any new business, the first few years were tumultuous, even resulting in a serious investigation of PCGS by the Federal Trade Commission. PCGS survived the investigation with a consent decree, and continued doing business and developing their market penetration.

Now, more than 25 years later, PCGS and NGC combined have graded literally tens of millions of coins and are reliable enough such that thousands of certified coins worth millions of dollars regularly change hands sight unseen.

In addition to grading coins, both PCGS and NGC created population reports that listed how many of each coin was certified at each grade level. At first, when only a few coins had been graded, their population reports were interesting, but of limited practical value because they represented only a small percentage of all gradable coins. Now, after a quarter century of record keeping, population figures are more useful. Population reports are available online at PCGS.com and NGCcoin.com.

The combination of accurate grading and population reports provides some of the most important information available to collectors and investors in the coin market today.

Take for example a 1925-S Peace dollar. In circulated grades, this is not a rare coin. In Very Good all the way to Extra Fine it has the same value as the 1922, which is the most common date Peace dollar. In MS-60, though, it climbs near to $100 — about double the price of a 1922 MS-60. In MS-63, the 1925-S climbs to the $225 to $250 range. In MS-64, it is in the $1,000 to $1,500 range, and in MS-65 — only one grade higher — it's worth close to $25,000!

How can one grade account for such a large difference in price? The population reports are enlightening. To date, PCGS has graded 1671 in MS-64 and only 36 coins in MS-65 with none better. NGC has graded 1536 in MS-64 and 59 in MS-65 with none better. The scarcity of the MS-65 relative to the MS-64 accounts for the big jump.

Of the nearly one hundred 1925-S Peace dollars that have achieved the grade of MS-65, some undoubtedly look better than others. Despite the advances made in grading consistency, grading is not 100-percent objective, and as mentioned above, experts will disagree about the grade of some coins.

Also, some factors not considered in determining the grade of the coin impact "eye appeal," and this in turn can impact value. Most disagreements about the grade of a PCGS or NGC certified coin usually come down to a discussion of whether the coin is "nice for the grade" or "not so nice for the grade." Generally speaking, the seller tends to think a coin is a little better than the buyer, often resolved by an adjustment in price.

To date, PCGS and NGC are the only two companies that guarantee the grades of their coins. They are also the only two that are accepted by the vast majority of dealers, meaning they have survived the test of the marketplace.

No grading system is perfect, though. From time to time, pretty much every dealer has had PCGS and NGC certified coins that in their opinion — and perhaps the opinion of an another with whom they might consult — are not accurately graded. As one might imagine, this can be infuriating.

Both PCGS and NGC have processes by which one can have a coin they feel is improperly graded reviewed. If it is determined that the coin is overgraded, the grading company insurance policy will buy the coin at the higher price.

What if you plain don't like the idea of PCGS or NGC reviewing their own work? The solution is terribly simple: break the plastic holder and have the coin graded again. There's no rule that says you can't. (The fact that coins can be graded multiple times can skew population report numbers.)

Indeed, there are opportunities to put your expert grading skills to task by scouring coin show displays, looking for coins that are so nice for the grade that they have the potential to be upgraded. If your perceptions are correct, you will be rewarded with more valuable coins. Many dealers, including myself, do this from time to time — with a good deal of success, I might add!

Naturally, this is at your own risk. Cracking a coin out of the holder effectively invalidates the insurance policy. Instead of being upgraded, a coin can be downgraded. Or, more likely, graded the same. In any case, there is the cost to grade a coin to consider, which averages $30 to $40 per coin, and more for particularly expensive coins or extra-fast service. When shipping and handling is added, these hard costs can add up fast. Plus, there is the time and energy that goes into hunting for these undergraded beauties. Remember, the graders at PCGS and NGC didn't just walk in off the street. Chances are if a slab reads MS-62, the coin really is an MS-62.

There is another grading company that deserves mention: Certified Acceptance Corporation. Unlike the other grading companies, CAC does not put coins into slabs. It only reviews already certified PCGS and NGC coins, and if CAC judges the coin to be at the top end of the range for that grade, they will put a green sticker on the slab. If the coin is superlative for the grade it would get a gold sticker. CAC certified coins tend to sell at a premium over non-CAC certified coins.

It makes very little sense to have PCGS or NGC certify a coin valued at $50 or less because

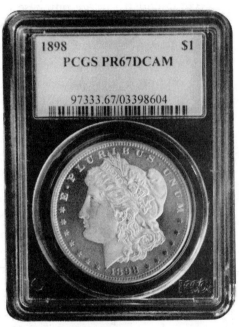

Photo courtesy Bill Goode

the cost of grading will boost one's effective purchase cost significantly above its value. On the other hand, if one buys a coin worth less than $50 that is already PCGS or NGC certified, the added value makes it a bargain.

One might wonder why such coins exist. After all, if a coin were worth less than $50, why would a dealer pay to get it certified? The answer is that they probably would not, but dealers are human too. They may have thought the coin would get a higher grade than PCGS or NGC actually awarded, leaving them with a loser which they often blow out for whatever they can get.

Also, both PCGS and NGC offer volume discounts when a dealer has scores or hundreds of coins to be graded at the same time. This is how most low-value certified coins find their way into the market.

On the other hand, for coins valued in excess of $100, especially where small differences in grade may greatly influence the value, it is recommended to *only* purchase coins that are certified by PCGS or NGC. This is even true after one becomes a competent grader. When it comes to buying expensive coins for clients, dealers almost always prefer to buy coins that are already certified by PCGS or NGC. It reduces not only the purchaser's risk, but the amount of time required, because a coin already certified is ready for sale, and does not require going through the process, time loss and expense of being sent to a grading company.

Second- and Third-Tier Grading Companies

PCGS and NGC are the industry wide acknowledged top-tier grading companies. There are other third-party grading services. ANACS has already been mentioned, which along with Independent Coin Graders are considered second tier because they do not guarantee either the grade or authenticity of the coins they grade. They tend to grade more liberally and less consistently than PCGS or NGC.

Some coins certified by ANACS or ICG have been broken out of their slabs, resubmitted to PCGS or NGC and received the same or better grades. Other coins certified by these two services, however, have been grossly overgraded. While these coins sometimes do sell sight unseen, the bids are often comparable to two or three grade levels below the bid value of PCGS or NGC certified coins.

ANACS seems to be taking steps to improve the accuracy and consistency of their grading, but they have not yet reached anywhere near the market acceptance level of PCGS or NGC. Also, ANACS is the only grading service which notates all the VAMs (die variations) for Morgan silver dollars. The grading fees for ANACS are less than PCGS or NGC, so for some collectors, ANACS certification is sufficient, especially if their main concern is establishing authenticity as opposed to the coin's grade.

ANACS in particular is a useful service for authentication and grading of circulated and problem coins, and tends to be used by collectors of low-end coins who want some assurance that their coins are genuine.

There are other grading services, including SEGS, NCI and Accugrade that coin dealers and knowledgeable collectors consider to be third-tier grading companies. Second-tier grading companies may not be as strict or consistent as PCGS or NGC. Third-tier grading companies, however, are frequently so far off the mark as to be essentially useless. In fact, they can be worse than useless. By giving the impression that a coin is a far higher grade than it actually is, third-tier grading companies can be used as a powerful sales tool for nefarious dealers.

Does this mean one should never buy a coin certified by a second- or third-tier company? Not necessarily. Sometimes coins certified by lower-tier grading companies are properly graded, truly lovely coins, or pretty coins with problems (cleaning, altered surface, rim nicks) which would enable the purchase of a desirable coin for a much lower price than a comparable PCGS or NGC coin.

Grading Modern Bullion Coins

Bullion coins are not generally graded because doing so is almost always a waste of money in that after paying $35 or more, plus mailing costs and taking the time to do so, it does not significantly raise the value of the coin. This is especially the case with most modern-issue gold and silver coins.

Yet, PCGS and NGC do fantastic business grading modern minted coins. The coin minting process is so excellent these days that pretty much every coin minted will be at least MS-67 or MS-68 quality. Though, in some cases, the sharp grading eyes at PCGS and NGC will certify modern coins as Mint State or Proof 69s and 70s. There are some people who will pay quite a premium for those coins.

Most collectors, including a fair number of experienced dealers, cannot tell the difference between an MS-69 and an MS-70.

Nonetheless, the simple fact that PCGS or NGC has graded the coin so high will frequently enable the coin to be sold for a premium — sometimes a hefty premium — above an ungraded-but-perfect-looking coin.

Mark Salzberg, Chairman of Numismatic Guaranty Corporation, grades a rare gold coin. *Photo courtesy NGC*

In recent years, many of these modern bullion coins graded MS-69 have dropped in price from their highs, while MS-70 coins seem, at least so far, to be holding their own. Whether that will continue is anyone's guess. Should people stop valuing the very slight differences between MS-70 coins and those in MS-69 or MS-68 grades, the premiums on the MS-70s would drop like a stone.

Unfortunately for many collectors of modern day numismatic coins, there is usually a huge difference between what dealers charge as a numismatic premium for MS-70 coins and what they are willing to pay for those coins when purchasing them back from the client. While this may be justified for some coins, it is an indication that the premium might be out of line in the long run. After all, these coins are not rare dates, and a huge quantity minted have not yet gone through the grading process, so it is likely that there are more MS-70s and MS-69s among them. If that were to happen, it would make MS-70s far more common, and they would likely see a corresponding drop in price.

It is also instructive that most experienced collectors are not buying MS-70 modern coins. Most of the action in that area, and certainly the enthusiasm, seems to be coming from those new to the business.

Whether big premiums for modern MS-70 coinage will stand the test of time is impossible to say, but history and the odds do not favor it. That said, because certified grading is so new, we are to some degree in uncharted territory. If market intelligence comes to value modern MS-70 and PR-70 coins over the long haul, these neophyte collectors might someday be considered prescient.

Eye Appeal

Grading is largely a technical exercise, and while it is essential in determining the value of a coin, there are other factors that do not impact the technical grade but can impact the market value. One of the most important is *eye appeal.*

Grading factors like luster, dings, cuts, scratches, rim nicks, cleaning or tooling can all be identified objectively. In contrast, eye appeal is at least partly subjective because it involves aesthetics. Some coins just look nicer than others. Maybe its marks are a bit less conspicuous than marks on another similarly graded coin. Or perhaps two coins have about the same level of wear, but the wear on one coin is perfectly even, whereas it is inconsistent or splotchy on another. Such coins could legitimately be awarded the same grade, but the one that is evenly worn will likely sell faster and for more.

Sometimes the grade given is a compromise. For example, the luster on a coin might justify an MS-65 grade, but there are so many marks that the coin cannot in good conscience be graded above MS-63. Or the luster might not be quite as good as most MS-64s, but there are so few marks that the grade is justified.

While even an unpracticed eye can make comparison judgments, it generally takes a fair amount of experience to understand what aesthetics are more commonly accepted and desired in the numismatic market. This is especially true when confronted with coins that have an aesthetic that is necessarily valued by collectors. One of these is *toning.*

Toning

Coins are made of metal, and most metals are subject to the chemical process known as *oxidation*. This process can change the color of a coin, sometimes radically. Even so, toning is *not* a factor used to determine the grade of a coin. This may seem odd because sometimes toning can be so dark and ugly that not to include it as a factor in grading seems to be intuitiviely wrong. Nevertheless, toning is not part of the grading criteria.

Attractive toning can actually be a plus to some people. Morgan dollars and early U.S. $.50 commemoratives sometimes tone in amazing displays of rainbow green, blue, gold and purple. Such coins can sometimes fetch several times the value of a non-toned, properly graded blast white coins.

While toning does not technically affect the grade, it does affect the eye appeal of a coin. If you are considering buying a toned coin, make sure it is attractively toned. Such toning rarely detracts from the value of a coin. Be careful, however, because taste in toning seems to improve with experience. Look at a lot of toned examples and talk to several dealers before paying a premium for toned coins, or even paying ordinary market prices for ugly toning.

This 1908 No Motto was one of 9900 gem quality $20 St. Gaudens discovered in the early 1990s. The largest hoard of its kind, thousands of the coins graded MS-66, almost 1000 graded MS-67, just over 100 were graded MS-68, only 10 graded MS-69 and despite close scrutiny by PCGS, not a single coin graded MS-70.

Ugly toning is when the toning is so dark it obstructs or limits the ability to view the coin's design, or if it is splotchy and inconsistent, or consists of one or more big spots. A small amount of even toning across the entire surface of the coin is generally no problem.

The Strike

Sometimes a coin will exhibit a *strong strike*, meaning the details of the design are exceptionally clear. In contrast, a coin may have a *weak* or *flat strike*. Usually these differences are attributable to whether the coin was struck when the die was new, or after it had struck thousands of coins and lost some of its crispness. Generally speaking, a stronger strike makes the coin more desirable. Yet, the quality of the strike is another factor that is not considered for the grade.

This is an issue that is important for some coins. For example, because of the way they were minted, Morgan silver dollars minted in New Orleans ("O" mintmark) tend to be struck with such flat strikes that to the unpracticed eye, they appear worn. Thus, when one finds an "O" mint Morgan dollar that has an exceptionally strong strike, it may be a coin that will sell at a premium.

The reverse is true for San Francisco minted — "S" mint — silver dollars, which characteristically exhibit not only a sharp strike but proof-like appearances as well.

That said, common date coins from both mints in the same grades sell for pretty much the same money, as the aforementioned characteristics have been accounted for in the marketplace.

While of interest for some collectors, and certainly when it comes to coins of high grade and great rarity, the impact of the strike quality on price for investment-oriented individuals buying mainly bullion, bullion-related coins, or generic gold and silver is of no practical consequence.

Originality and Coin Doctoring

Having an original look is highly valued among most coin collectors. What *original* really means, however, is that the coin has never been messed with. When a coin has been sufficiently altered in order to improve its eye appeal, it is considered to be *doctored*.

This generally does not include such simple treatment as rinsing a coin in water, or so-called light or minor cleaning.

The Professional Numismatists Guild has defined coin doctoring in the following way:

> "Coin doctoring refers to the alteration of any portion of a coin, when that process includes any of the following: 1) Movement, addition to, or otherwise altering of metal, so that a coin appears to be in a better state of preservation, or more valuable than it otherwise would be. A few examples are plugging, whizzing, polishing, engraving, "lasering" and adding or removing mint marks. 2) Addition of any substance to a coin so that it appears to be in a better state of preservation or more valuable than it otherwise would be. The use of solvents and/or commercially available dilute acids, such as Jeweluster, by qualified professionals is not considered coin doctoring. 3) Intentional exposure of a coin to any chemicals, substances, or processes which impart toning, such that the coin appears to be in a better state of preservation or more valuable than it otherwise would be. Naturally occurring toning imparted during long-term storage using established/traditional methods, such as coin albums, rolls, flips, or envelopes, does not constitute coin doctoring."

As is apparent, there is a gray area when it comes to cleaning. Sometimes a properly, or lightly, cleaned coin will lose some of its original look when compared to coins that have never had any cleaning or any chemical applied to them.

Or, conversely, because of the way a coin has been preserved over the long term, it may develop a unique and attractive character that establishes it as highly original. Such coins often, but not always, attract more buyers and a higher price.

Grading is a complicated issue, and the more one knows, the more complex it seems to become. For most collectors and investors, it is not necessary to become a superb grader. What is necessary is to know enough about it to keep from making serious and costly mistakes.

Chapter Five

Pricing

ONE OF THE BIGGEST CONCERNS PEOPLE have, especially when they first explore the area of rare coins or precious metals, is how to make sure they get good prices when they buy or sell. People, quite naturally, don't want to be ripped off.

It is a valid concern, but before addressing the technical aspects of pricing coins, it is necessary to look at the mental attitudes relating to buying and selling. The approach one takes is just as important as market information when it comes to making good deals.

Psychology of Buying and Selling

No one likes to pay too much, or sell for too little. Of course, most people want the exact opposite — that's human nature. However, when pressed, most people are content with a fair deal. People generally define a "fair" price as the price a reasonable and knowledgeable person would pay or accept for a certain item at a certain time.

The reality is that those parameters can vary from person to person and circumstance to circumstance.

For example, dealers will rarely pay as much for a single coin as a private collector who wants that coin, because they cannot afford to do so and stay in business. On the other hand, a dealer can usually pay a great deal more than a private collector for a large accumulation. This is because a dealer has a wide array of buyers for almost any type of material. He can flip a wide variety of diverse coins and quickly recoup his funds, making a small but sure profit on every part of the accumulation. A private collector on the other hand may not want most of the items in an accumulation, and lacks the resources to quickly resell the items he does not want.

In one case, the seller could get more for his coin from a private collector. In the other case, he would get more from a dealer. So what is the fair price? Is it the one the dealer would pay, or the one the private collector would pay?

Dealers also vary in their financial resources, and in the range and variety of potential buyers in their network. Some dealers will pay more than others, depending on the material involved. So which is the fair price?

A knowledgeable and reasonable collector might well pay more for a superlative coin, or exemplary service, or for ease and reliability in transactions. Is it an unfair price if there are other places from which he might obtain the same coin in the same grade for less but without the service, reliability or convenience?

Regardless of what a collector or dealer might pay, the seller might have a completely different definition of fair than either a dealer or another collector.

Because prices fluctuate, a fair price yesterday may not be a fair price today, which in turn may not be a fair price tomorrow. A dealer might be willing to sell something at a lower price today because he needs to generate capital, and then raise his price the next day because a check he thought was delayed actually arrived on time.

When a fair price has so much elasticity, how can we define it?

The simple fact is that the same coin can legitimately be bought or sold at a wide variety of prices at the same time. For example, let's say a dealer buys a coin from a client for $2,000. Let's say he does not have a customer for that coin, so he sells it to another dealer for $2,100. The reason the other dealer bought the coin is that he has a buyer willing to pay $2,600 for the coin.

This could all happen with the space of a few days, a few hours, or even a few minutes, and yet, the legitimate price for the coin varied by about 30 percent. Was it fair that one person could buy it for $2,000 while another would have to pay $2,600? And what is the legitimate price for that coin? Is it $2,000, or is it $2,600?

Beyond the practicalities of determining fair, approaching the issue of coin pricing from that perspective does not help one buy coins for less or sell them for more. There will always be a range of price levels at which coins can legitimately be bought or sold that does not depend on objective pricing information, but rather on circumstances related to the specific needs of buyers and sellers. If one focuses attention to what is fair, one risks spending time and energy trying to "look into other people's pockets," rather than focusing on the actual value one gets or receives.

Since dealers arguably buy and sell more coins more frequently than anyone else, and have their business on the line while doing it, a peek into the dealers' point of view is instructive. The dealer by necessity must look at everything not from a what-is-fair perspective, but rather from a gross-profit perspective. Whether or not someone is being fair is of much less importance than getting or receiving sufficient value for the coins he buys and sells and for the time, energy and expense he expends on the transaction. Thus, when a dealer pays $2,000 for a coin from a client, it wasn't because he thought it was a fair deal but because he could resell that coin either to a customer or to another dealer for more than what he paid, enough to make executing the transaction worthwhile.

When he sold that coin to another dealer for $2,100, he made his profit and now is ready to make more purchases. The price at which the other dealer resells the coin does not matter. Nor does he care what the person from whom he bought the coin originally paid for it. He is focused on one thing: current value.

That is a powerful posture to adopt, because instead of wasting time and energy and risking high blood pressure judging whether or not someone is being fair, it allows one to focus exclusively on the value of a coin, and whether the deal is a good one for them. Instead of worrying about being ripped off, one can focus on digesting relevant market information about coin values through the lens of one's specific goals and needs. This gives one an advantage whether buying or selling.

Regardless of how much knowledge one might have about the market, some deals will be better than others. This is as true for professional dealers as it is for individuals. The real question is one of value: How to get good value when buying and selling? Obviously, it is important to consult the best market information and price parameters available to determine if the offer under consideration is a good value for one's purposes. This functions somewhat differently when it comes to precious metals than it does for numismatic coins, so we will examine each separately.

Determining Value for Precious Metals

To get good value when buying gold or silver — or other precious metals for that matter — it is necessary to know the following:

- The current spot or melt price of the metal
- The retail spread
- The cost of delivery

Fortunately, this information is easily obtained. For the spot price of gold, silver, platinum or palladium, simply consult any reliable media outlet, or online commodity trader. There are many of these, and they can be found by using a search engine and typing in something like "gold spot price" or "silver spot price." This information is also available in most daily newspapers, radio and other media.

Knowing the current spot price is obviously critical, as that is the single largest component of the total price. In a perfect world, if the spot price of silver is $30 an ounce, one would be able to buy and sell silver at that price. And in fact that is possible if one buys and sells silver using paper instruments, such as an ETF. With physical possession however, there are other costs that must be taken into account, specifically the spread and delivery costs.

What is the Spread?

Before getting into detail about spreads, it is important to know why they are so essential and how they function when it comes to buying and selling bullion.

If one buys and sells through a professional dealer, it is a foregone conclusion that the dealer will make a profit on each transaction. That profit is called the spread. It is what enables dealers to be ready on short notice to buy and sell at the convenience of the client. If there was no spread there would be no dealers, and then, if one wanted to sell an ounce of gold, it would require not only finding a private buyer, but one willing to pay the price desired. Private buyers who don't have a reputation to uphold or who do not care about future business might offer far less for gold and silver than a professional who knows how to quickly flip the material for a sure, if modest, profit. Moreover, to function effectively, dealers must have sufficient cash liquidity available to handle whatever deals come their way. Dealers and the spreads they make facilitate faster and convenient trading, which saves people time, stress, and frequently, costs of sale. In exchange for those advantages, the dealer makes his profit on the spread.

Buy/Sell Spread

Perhaps the most basic spread is the buy/sell spread, which refers to the total difference between the buy and sell prices of a particular item at a particular time. With regard to the physical trading in precious metals, there are two kinds of buy-sell spreads: one retail, and one wholesale.

While it does not directly impact most individual transactions, it is useful to understand that like a retail dealer who provides a service to the public in being available to quickly and conveniently transact purchases and sales, there are wholesale dealers who provide that service for retail coin and bullion dealers. The spreads charged retail dealers by wholesale dealers for gold, for example, usually run between one to two percent, and is sandwiched between the retail spread, which typically runs around six to seven percent. Thus, the retail buy price is lower than the wholesale buy price, and the retail sell price is higher than the wholesale sell price.

To illustrate, suppose the spot price for gold is $1,200 an ounce. Dealers buying from the public might pay $1,176, so they can sell to a wholesaler at $1,212, grossing a profit of $36 an ounce. The same retail dealer might sell to the public for $1,260, for a buy/sell spread of $84, or roughly 6 percent.

$1,260/oz — Retail Sale Price (spot +5%): The price retail dealers sell to the public

$1,230/oz — Retail Dealer Purchase Price (spot +2.5%): The price retail dealers buy from wholesale dealers

$1,212/oz — Wholesale Purchase Price (spot +1%): The price wholesale dealers buy from retail dealers

$1,200/oz — Spot Gold

$1,176/oz — Retail Purchase Price (spot -2%): The price retail dealers buy from the public

Example of wholesale and retail dealers' spreads based on gold at $1,200/oz. The size of these spreads are not limited or regulated by law. Percentages represented here are typical, but actual spreads can vary.

Because people are tyically not buying and selling at the same time, the spread often refers only to one side — either the buyer's side or the seller's side — of the total buy/sell spread. There is no fixed formula about what portion of the total buy/sell spread must be above or below the spot price — the spread above or below spot can and will vary day to day, according to market conditions, dealer cash and inventory levels, and customer supply and demand. There are spreads with virtually every kind of bullion product, and they all operate in similar fashion.

This is nothing new. When the U.S. government first started minting silver and gold coins, they kept some of the metal to finance the cost of minting and distribution. That is why each dollar in face value of U.S. 90-percent silver coins has only .723 ounces of silver. It is also why each $20 in face value of gold coins only contains .9650 ounces of pure gold.

This continues today, except instead of taking some of the metal from each ounce, the Mint charges a premium on top of the metal's per ounce cost. The following is quoted from the website of the U.S. Mint (December 2012):

"The United States Mint charges a modest premium above the current market price of platinum, gold, and silver to cover minting, distribution and marketing costs.

- For the Silver Eagle, we charge the United States Mint's Authorized Purchasers the price of silver plus $2.00 per coin premium. Minimum ordering requirement is 25,000 coins.
- For the Gold Eagles, we charge 3%, 5%, 7% and 9% premiums for the one, one-half, one-quarter and one-tenth ounce coins respectively. Minimum ordering requirements are 1,000 ounces.
- For the Platinum Eagles, we charge 4%, 6%, 10% and 15% premiums for the one, one-half, one-quarter and one-tenth ounces coins respectively. Minimum ordering requirements are 1,000 ounces."

The products referred to above are not offered by the Mint directly to individuals, so the only way individuals can buy these products is through dealers. Naturally, authorized purchasers, who are wholesale dealers, add an additional premium above what the Mint charges them. Note also the minimum buying requirements: 25,000 coins for silver and 1,000 ounces for gold. Unless they are bullion specialists, most retail dealers do not have the customer base or trading platform for those quantities. However, wholesale dealers, by servicing numerous retail dealers, can purchase directly from the Mint and move massive quantities of product. Trading in large volume enables wholesale bullion dealers to be profitable even with very small spreads.

What about when individuals want to resell their precious metals? The U.S. Mint won't buy them back. Retail dealers fulfill that role, and wholesale dealers make it easy for retail dealers to do so. For example, if a monster box of American silver eagles (500 one-ounce coins) cost spot plus $2 per coin from the Mint, a wholesaler might resell a monster box to a retail dealer at spot plus $2.50 per coin and might buy from a retail dealer at spot plus $1.50. The wholesale buy/sell spread would therefore be $1 per ounce, which, if silver is $30 per ounce, roughly amounts to a 3-percent wholesale spread.

Retail dealers know that if they need to sell to a wholesaler they can sell for spot price plus $1.50 per coin. Therefore, when they buy from customers, they need to pay a price that enables them to profit if they quickly flip the deal to a wholesaler. Thus, for American silver eagles, dealers may pay anywhere from spot price to several dollars below spot depending on the market and other conditions, such as the size of the purchase, the location where purchased, the cost of purchase, the condition of the coins, and so forth.

The base cost to retailers starts at $2.50 over spot price, but can sometimes be $2.75, $3.00 or more above spot depending on market conditions. Retailers then add an additional premium to cover their costs and make a profit.

There are some dealers who try to cut the spread, but the problem is that there are fixed costs such as time, funds transfer and delivery that must also be paid. Furthermore, should the price change on the gold or silver — and prices certainly can be volatile — dealers can actually lose money on a transaction, which adds an element of risk. The existence of wholesalers in the bullion markets enables dealers to effectively manage risk while working within a small spread, which provides better service and better prices for the public.

Because virtually all retail dealers can access the wholesale markets, and because they must remain competitive in order to attract business, there is usually little difference in the spreads charged by retail dealers on bullion transactions. There are exceptions. Some dealers have been known to charge exorbitant spreads when buying and selling. It is up to the individual consumer to remain vigilant about what spreads are being charged.

Certain factors legitimately affect the size of the spread, of course. One of these is the size of the transaction. Dealers will often charge a smaller percentage on a 1,000-ounce silver deal than on a three-ounce one, because there are minimum costs associated with any deal, regardless of the quantity.

Spreads can also vary depending on the ease of doing the transaction. If a dealer buys a quantity of silver at a coin show, then sells, delivers and receives payment at the same venue — when packing and shipping are not involved — he may be able to work a on a smaller spread.

The important thing to remember is that the spreads for bullion and bullion related-coins are generally between five to 15 percent (depending on coin denominations). Premiums on bullion or bullion coins that approach or exceed 20 percent above the spot price are almost certainly excessive.

Spreads for scrap gold or jewelry gold are much larger and will vary between dealers. Most dealers will pay between 60 to 80 percent of scrap melt value. Many dealers prefer not to deal with scrap and discourage that business with ridiculously low offers.

The important thing to remember when it comes to scrap gold is that the purity of the gold matters. Twenty-four carat gold is pure. Twelve carat gold is 50 percent pure. Therefore, at $1,700 per ounce, an ounce of 24 carat gold has a melt value of $1,700, and 12 carat gold has a melt value of $850.

Delivery Costs

Finally, it is important to know the terms and costs of delivery. Unless one physically picks up or drops off the coins or bars, additional charges for shipping effectively add to the spread paid on the metal. With gold, this is rarely an issue, but with silver, because of its weight and volume, it can be a significant expense.

Sometimes, spreads can be negotiable. Say one wishes to purchase 100 American silver eagles. The client asks the dealer the spread, and the dealer says: "Spot plus $6 per coin." The client might then respond: "If I purchase a monster box of 500 American silver eagles can you charge me spot plus $4?" And the dealer might counter: "I can charge you spot plus $5 on a monster box, but only if you either pay for shipping, or pick it up personally, and only if I receive good funds the day before by bank wire."

After determining whether this is the best deal, the client then will choose to execute the trade or not. Sometimes, an individual will use the knowledge of one offer to negotiate a favorable exchange with another dealer.

Determining Values for Numismatic Coins

With precious metals, where price is based on metal content, determining spreads and value is relatively simple and straightforward. With numismatic coins, however, the price is determined by a long list of variables. These include precious metals content, grade, rarity, market conditions, the urgency of the sale, the type of coins, the peculiarities of the specific coins involved, the cash needs of the dealer, the dealers' relationship with the client, how many coins and dollars are involved, whether the coins are raw or certified, the amount of work required to process coins for resale among many others. It comes as no surprise that spreads cannot operate in a consistent way or at a standard percentage in this kind of environment.

Spreads exist nonetheless, as that is the difference in price between what a dealer will pay for a coin, and the price for which he is willing to sell it. Spread amounts and percentages are radically inconsistent because in the numismatic market every coin and every deal is different. Dealers are usually more interested in receiving value for time, expenses, profit, and the cost of capital expended than on making a specific percentage or spread.

The average spread runs in the neighborhood of 15 to 30 percent for most smaller dealers and as much as 40 to 50 percent for some of the larger dealers with more overhead. But these percentages are only guidelines and exceptions are common.

While it is essential to be mindful that there is a spread when it comes to buying and selling coins, it is superfluous to try to look into a dealer's pocket and worry about how much he is making on the deal.

It is much more important for the client to know how to determine if the transaction is a good value. While vast trading experience or knowledge about all coins may not be necessary, specific knowledge of the pricing parameters about the exact coin one is selling or buying is essential.

Fortunately, the necessary information is well organized and readily available in the form of price guides and population reports. Even someone with relatively little knowledge or experience can buy or sell with a fair degree of confidence if he knows what to look for.

Price Guides

One issue not covered in outlining key differences between the coin market and the stock market is pricing. The values of stocks are based on actual trades that have occurred, and the spreads between the bid and ask prices exist in real time. The stock market is highly controlled, and trades go through a central exchange where prices are reported publically and available to everyone.

In contrast, there is no centralized exchange for numismatic coins. Instead, the vast majority of numismatic buys and sells take place privately, and these trades are not required to be reported to a central authority. The only somewhat centralized exchange is the Certified Coin Exchange, where only a fraction of dealer-to-dealer transactions are reported, mostly for what are known as *generic* coins — common date coins of the same denomination, date and grade that trade in relatively large volumes.

Most dealers are not involved in that kind of trading, so the majority of their activity with other dealers and their clients remains private. Consequently, there is no precise information about what trades have occurred in real time that can in any significant way compare to the trading mechanisms of the stock market.

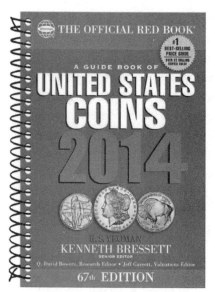

2014 Red Book. *Image used with permission.* © *Whitman Publishing, LLC. All Rights Reserved*

Auctions are the exception, but since the vast majority of coins are not sold through auction, the value of knowing a particular transaction price is not always an accurate barometer of the overall marketplace. Moreover, auction prices can vary depending on a wide variety of issues, including the location of the auction, who runs it, who attends, and the degree to which the coins sold are "weak" or "strong" for the grade. Even unrelated current events or bad weather can influence the prices paid for auctioned coins.

This leaves price guides as the best price references readily available for numismatic coins.

Price guides were originally compiled by dealers, collectors or scholars and published in a book or pamphlet and, at least in the beginning, were published sporadically. Then, with the advent of rare coin magazines, prices were published monthly.

The information inside these guides were not necessarily based on actual sales prices. They included advertised prices for certain coins, anecdotal knowledge of the person assembling the pricing information, and commentary by dealers and experienced collectors surveyed at coin shows. Sometimes they were little more than educated guesses.

As the decades rolled on, more price guides appeared. They were published more frequently and, with the advent of the internet, price sheets became digital and subject to much more rapid adjustment than annual or monthly price guides could ever provide.

While they are not perfect, price guides are perhaps the best means of determining the current market value of a coin. Dealers use them extensively. Three important points about price sheets must be kept in mind. First, they are usually based on information that is at least a week old. Second, because of the way price information is gathered, they are far from perfect, and the prices of actual sales can vary, sometimes significantly, from the prices found in price guides.

Third, all price guides are not created equal. This is especially true because of the internet, which allows virtually anyone, whether knowledgeable or not, to create a price guide. Sometimes these price guides are created by the very people selling the highlighted coins, with a tendency to publish wildly exaggerated prices. Others have been created by people who buy coins, which are unrealistically low. There are some price sheets that have no relation to reality whatsoever.

Knowing which price sheets to use is therefore essential.

A good methodology involves consulting several different price sheets to determine the current price range for a particular coin. Price ranges by definition are not specific and accurate the way stock prices are, but knowing the high and low prices of a certain coin provides the flexibility so that visual or aesthetic differences can be accommodated.

Using the price range to determine a coin's value as opposed to a specific price has many advantages. First, it enables one to adjust price according to current market conditions, the specifics of the coin involved, such as its eye appeal or particular look. Second, it reflects the elasticity of price that exists in the market. Third, it can warn against paying too much or accepting too little for a particular coin. Finally, it can also provide useful market information, but only if they are effectively interpreted.

The following are the most prominent retail price guides for U.S. coins in today's market, and they are the ones which this author primarily consults:

- *The Red Book: A Guide Book of United States Coins* (Whitman) — published annually
- *Coin World* magazine — published monthly online and print
- PCGS price guide — updated daily at www.pcgs.com
- NGC price guide — updated daily at www.ngccoins.com

Using Price Guides Effectively

The first step in determining value is to establish the grade of the coin in question. All price guides list different prices for each coin depending on the grade, and if one does not know the grade of a coin, it is impossible to use price guides effectively.

When the grade of a coin is established by either of the two premier grading services — PCGS and NGC — the process is simplified, although there might still be some elasticity in the prices based on whether the coin is nice for the grade or weak for the grade. While they might differ somewhat in price due to such variables as eye appeal, toning, or minor variances of condition within the grade itself coins of the same mint, denomination and grade usually sell within a fairly narrow price range.

Raw coins tend to sell for less than PCGS or NGC certified coins. When coins are *raw* or uncertified, one should be a knowledgeable grader or get the assistance of one. This is obviously more important when dealing with expensive coins than with low-priced common circulated coins.

The companies that publish price guides encourage dealers to pay for advertising or use their services. As such these relationships are perhaps too cozy. As dealers are among the main promoters, prices listed in the retail guides are designed to enable them to make a profit. Still, this desire to please dealers is balanced by the fact that retail guides are in competition with each other. It is in their best interest to cultivate and maintain a reputation for accuracy and reliability in order to increase their market share of consumers, to whom they hope to sell their publication and other products.

In any event, prices in the aforementioned retail guides are not trading levels like stock prices. They are retail prices. One cannot purchase coins at retail prices and expect to flip the coin for a profit in the short term.

While dealers are ordinarily happy to sell at listed retail prices, they will not buy at those levels — not if they wish to stay in business. Indeed, individuals can almost always buy coins from dealers at or close to the price levels printed in the retail guides, because by selling at those levels coin dealers can virtually be assured to make a profit. Since dealers know this in advance, they know what they can reasonably pay — or not pay — when buying. Many individuals do not grasp this basic fact, which is why pretty much every dealer has been approached by someone holding a *Coin World* magazine, or a price listed on the PCGS website on their iPad, expecting the dealer to pay those prices for his coins. Such folks are bound to be disappointed.

As a rule of thumb, it is wise never to pay more for a coin than the retail price as listed in these guides. This cannot be a fast and hard rule, however, because the price guides differ from each other on various coins. These inconsistencies make using a price range, rather than a specific price the most effective approach to price sheets. It is also why consulting several guides is such a good idea.

Wholesale Price Guides

There are fewer wholesale price guides than retail price guides — mainly because publishers tend to cater to the larger coin collecting public rather than to dealers. Reliable price guides are consumer publications. Whatever the reason, wholesale price guides provide an additional perspective to the price range of a coin, and this applies whether one is buying or selling.

By far the least expensive and most available wholesale price guide is the *Handbook of United States Coins*, commonly known as the *Blue Book* — the companion price guide to the *Red Book*. Instead of publishing retail prices, the *Blue Book* publishes *dealer-buy* prices.

Therefore, one good and simple method for establishing the price range of a coin is to look up prices in both books and compare. Usually, the *Blue Book* price will be approximately half of the *Red Book* price. There are exceptions, especially for generic gold coins, and other coins that derive most or all of their value from their gold or silver content.

This does not mean that dealers will only buy at the prices published in the *Blue Book*. Just like the retail guides publish prices at which dealers can be assured of making a profit, prices published in the *Blue Book* are designed so that dealers buying at that level are sure to make a profit when they resell. The most valuable use of the *Blue Book* is that it reveals what is likely the minimum legitimate sell price for an individual coin. Just like it is unadvisable to purchase a coin at prices higher than the retail price guides, it is also advisable in most cases not to sell for lower than *Blue Book* prices.

The other wholesale price guide is used almost exclusively by dealers and other numismatic professionals. It is called the *Coin Dealer Newsletter*, better known as the *Grey Sheet*. The *Coin Dealer Newsletter* also publishes a *Blue Sheet* that lists bid prices on the certified wholesale dealer-to-dealer exchanges, and a *Green Sheet* that focuses on U.S. bank notes. Subscriptions to these price sheets cost hundreds of dollars per year, and take a fair amount of practice and experience to use properly. Moreover, even if one has this price information and understands how to use it, it may not help obtain lower prices. Generally speaking, dealers cannot afford to sell to their retail customers at *Grey Sheet* prices and still stay in business.

The spread between bid and ask prices on the *Grey Sheet* is small because it is designed for trades between dealers. Dealers cannot make any money at those price levels unless they buy and sell a large volume, or if they are flipping a coin or a group of coins. In this case, the word "flip" means something similar to what it means in the real estate business, when people buy a piece of real estate and flip it, making a small but predictable profit on a fast sale.

Furthermore, prices in the *Grey Sheet*, just like prices in the retail guides and the *Blue Book* are only guidelines and estimates. It is not uncommon for actual trades between dealers to take place above or below price levels appearing in the *Grey Sheet*, again, depending on the peculiarities of the individual coin involved, market conditions and the supply and demand needs of the dealers involved in the transaction.

There are far too many coins to provide a comprehensive application of these price guides to every coin. For our purposes here, it is far more important to understand the thinking process as applied to price sheets, and how they can be used effectively to determine current market values, and more importantly, how to obtain good values when buying or selling.

The prices used in the following examples are from the *2013 Red Book*; the November, 2012 edition of *Coin World*; and listed January 10, 2013 on the PCGS and NGC websites.

Say you are thinking of purchasing a 1916-D Mercury dime, graded EF-40 and selling for $6,500. You check the above price guides and find the following:

- *Red Book*: $6,200
- *Coin World*: $6,000
- PCGS: $5,750
- NGC: $5,940
- *Blue Book*: $2,750
- *Grey Sheet*: bid $5,250 / ask $5,650

All four retail guides list prices within a range of $5750 to $6200, for a spread of $450, or about 8 percent. That is a fairly narrow price range. But the offered price of the coin is five percent above the highest retail price listed, and $500 above the average. It would appear at first glance that $6,500 is too high.

However, since the *Grey Sheet* price is so close to the prices in the retail guides, it is possible this coin is a good value even at $6,500, especially since it is the key date in the Mercury Dime series. If the coin is CAC stickered or has a "+" addendum, indicating it is superlative for the grade, the price becomes even more attractive.

Now say the same coin is offered at $7,500. Here the price is so far above the retail guides that it suggests the person offering it has an inflated idea of the coin's value. It would have to be an outstanding example to justify that price, and even then it is probably a stretch. Still, the *Grey Sheet* price is only about 10 percent lower than the average of the retail guides, which indicates the true retail price for this coin might be well above retail price guide levels.

A useful question the buyer should then ask himself is at what price level could he reasonably expect to sell the coin if it already owned it?

The *Blue Book* price is $2,750, so that would certainly be a minimum price. Yet with *Grey Sheet* prices averaging around $5,500, it would be reasonable to assume that if a dealer needed to make 20 percent on the coin he would likely pay around $4,000 to $4,500 for the coin, possibly more if he has a customer who wants that coin.

Thus, one can establish that the effective price range for a PCGS or NGC certified 1916-D Mercury dime in EF-40 is approximately $4,000 to $6,500.

The buyer can now shop with confidence from a value standpoint, taking into account the look of a coin, how nice it is for the grade, and how important it is to him to own it. If he's smart, he might point out that the retail price guides are less than the price offered and ask if the dealer has "any room" in the price. If the answer is maybe, an offer in the $6000 to $6,200 range might well result in a purchase.

Let's take another example, this time for a coin that has wide variance among the retail price guides: the 1893-CC $5 Liberty Gold, MS-60 offered at $2,500.

- *Red Book*: $2,000
- *Coin World*: $2,650
- PCGS: $2,500
- NGC: $1,910
- *Blue Book*: $1,150
- *Grey Sheet*: $1,250

Two of the retail guides list the coin at $2,500 to $2,600, and two list it at $1,900 to $2,000. Like the previous examples, the *Blue Book* is around 50 percent of the lower retail price guides, and the *Grey Sheet* is slightly above the *Blue Book*.

What does this tell us? First, there is a wide spread — more than 25 percent — between the retail guides, which indicates prices for this coin may be in flux. Now note that the *Red Book*, whose prices are much older than the other three guides, is the lowest retail estimate. The likelihood is that this coin is rising in value.

But that's not the end of the story. Both the *Blue Book* and *Grey Sheet* prices are barely more than 50 percent of the NGC and *Red Book* prices, indicating the higher prices listed by PCGS and *Coin World* are out of whack. *Blue Book* prices at just 40 percent of the high retail prices appears to be too low.

This kind of disparity is a caution flag. What can account for the difference?

A quick check of Collectors Corner — or one can use another online auction site — shows two 1893-CC $5 for sale: an XF-45 at $675 and an MS-62 at $3,870. An MS-60 is close to the center of that range, but it does not help us determine if the price of the 1893-CC in MS-60 should be around $2,500 or closer to $2,000. We should keep investigating.

Jewish War (66-70 A.D.) AR Shekel, Year 1, realized $1,105,375 at auction. *Photo courtesy Heritage Auctions (www.ha.com)*

Checking on the PCGS.com Coin Facts service ($99 per year or $12.95 per month; NGC also has excellent coin information offered at no cost), we see there are no current auction prices for this coin. The closest current auction prices are for an 1893-CC in MS-61, and those prices range from a low of $1,900 to a high of $6,325, with many prices in between.

The MS-61 price range, as is often the case with auction figures, is hardly definitive but it does indicate that some coins are much better for the grade, or possibly under graded. Still, that also does not provide a strong value indicator for an MS-60. We should keep investigating.

The wholesale price guides — the *Blue Book* and *Grey Sheet* — are fairly close, which means that more than likely if one had an 1893-CC coin to sell, most dealers would offer in the neighborhood of $1100 for that coin, a bit behind the *Grey Sheet*. Even at the lower range of retail price guides, that represents a significant spread. One has to ask if the 1893-CC $5 MS-60 is something we want enough to pay $2,500, when we know that currently we could only sell it at less than half the price?

Korea: Yung Hi Gold 20 Won, Year 3 (1909), in MS-64 (NGC) realized $3,172,500 at auction. *Photo courtesy Heritage Auctions (www.ha.com)*

The answer is probably no, but still, this does not make a whole lot of sense — until we notice that the PCGS population report lists that PCGS has only graded five coins in MS-60 while having graded many more, 31, in MS-61. Checking the NGC census, we see 11 coins graded in MS-60, with 50 graded in MS-61.

Now we know the problem: There are not enough sale examples to create a strong price indicator in the MS-60 grade, because, with a total of only 16 graded, it is unlikely one would ever encounter this exact coin, and it is possible that none have even sold in recent years! Indeed, one is far more likely to encounter an MS-61.

The low auction price of an MS-61 at $1,900 combined with the roughly $1,100 price level of both wholesale guides indicates that paying $2,500 for an MS-60 is probably a risky move, because when going to sell, the wholesale price is so much lower. However, if one were to come across a nice MS-60 1893-CC $5 coin selling at $1,900, it could be an excellent value.

It may take some practice to develop one's facility in analyzing coins through this method, but knowledge is power and knowing and using this information will usually prevent one from making any serious mistakes when it comes to buying coins.

Auction Prices

The proliferation of online bidding at numismatic auctions, as well as auction sites like eBay has led more and more people to start considering auction results for determining the value of a specific type of coin. Usually, these prices will fall within the basic range of the various price guides, although sometimes, they will show prices that are higher or lower.

The advantage of consulting auction prices is that they show what someone else actually paid for a certain coin in a certain grade at a certain time. However, they have some disadvantages, which can be misleading when trying to establish value. First and foremost, auctions represent a tiny fraction of the overall market trading activity. Second, auction prices are affected by its specific bidding population — in other words, the pool of people that participate. Many dealers and the vast majority of coin buyers do not participate in auctions. Third, since coins of the same grade can differ in terms of

1913 5¢ Liberty in PR-63 (PCGS) realized $3,172,500 at auction. *Photo courtesy Heritage Auctions (www.ha.com)*

their eye appeal and by whether they are strong or weak for the grade, auction prices for coins of the same year, denomination and grade might sell for wildly diverse prices, as we saw with the 1893-CC $5 coin in MS-61. At some auctions, there may be very few bidders for a specific coin, or perhaps the reserve price is set high enough such that attendees feel discouraged from bidding at all. Thus, prices realized at auction reflect the market at that specific time and place only, and that may or may not be characteristic of the overall market.

Furthermore, one enthusiastic bidder — or someone who gets carried away by the excitement of an auction — can distort auction prices by paying way above market for a coin.

Thus, the downside of considering auction prices is that some people make the mistake of assuming that auction prices are the "real" price. People have passed up perfectly fine deals on excellent coins because one auction price listed was far lower than the price in the price guides. Conversely, some people have paid what might be considered exorbitant prices for coins that happened to have one or two high auction results. It is generally a good idea to throw out the highest and lowest auction results when evaluating the price range of a coin using auction results.

Austrian 100 Corona obverse and reverse. The Austrian 100 Corona and Hungarian 100 Korona are identical except the Austrian obverse has a Franz Joseph I profile and the Hungarian coin has him standing, holding a sphere and specter, and the reverse has the Hungarian Coat of Arms, a shield held by winged angels. Both coins contain .9802 of an ounce of pure gold.

Population Reports

Rarity is a key element of value for collectible coins. It is one reason why people spend so much time looking at mintage records. From the moment they were minted, dates with low mintages are rarer than coins with high mintages, and collectors will pay more for them. It used to be that mintage figures were the primary means of determining rarity. While mintage figures are still very important, a significant wrinkle has developed over the last 25 years, and it began with the inception of the

Professional Coin Grading Service, and came into full bloom with the Numismatic Guaranty Corporation.

In addition to strictly grading coins, one of the innovations developed by PCGS was the population report. The theory was that regardless of original mintage figures, true rarity was also impacted by the survival rate of coins, and by how many remained extant in various grades. PCGS figured rightly that customers would like to know how many coins were certified in each grade, so they kept track, and then published the results.

In the beginning this led to all sorts of confusion, because when only a few coins had been certified, some coins with relatively large populations might only have had a handful of examples certified, and would, at least for a time, appear to be rarer in the population reports than they actually were. Even now, after over 25 years, and with both PCGS and NGC issuing population information, these reports are far from perfect.

1907 $10 Satin in PR-67 (NGC) realized $2,185,00 at auction. *Photo courtesy Heritage Auctions (www.ha.com)*

Since they only list the coins they have actually certified and the number of coins certified in each grade, they do not include ungraded coins or coins graded by a competing grading service. Furthermore, they do not count coins that have been submitted more than once for grading, unless the submitting dealer or individual returns the paper tag inside the slab to the grading company. This can be a real problem because if a coin is on the cusp of a grade, and if the prices between grades justify it, some dealers might submit a coin again and again, sometimes to NGC and sometimes to PCGS, with the hope that at least once, it will receive the higher grade.

Each submission will be counted, so there are instances where the population reports actually list a higher count for certain dates and denominations than likely exist! As imperfect as they are, population reports provide information useful to determining a coin's value. This is especially true when considering expensive coins in high grades, because there are sometimes huge gaps in price between grade levels.

Using Population Reports and Price Sheets Together

Take for example, the 1922-S Peace dollar in MS-65 and MS-66. Retail prices listed in the four predominant price guides are as follows:

Source	MS-65	MS-66
Red Book	$2,500	$20,000
Coin World	$2,800	$18,500
PCGS	$2,100-3,850	$30,000
NGC	$1,880	$15,310

The price gap between MS-65 and MS-66 is huge, and the reason becomes clear by examining the PCGS and NGC populations reports. In MS-65, PCGS reports 286 graded, with only 7 in MS-66. NGC shows 253 graded in MS-65 and only 13 in MS-66.

While the population figures may not be perfect, they provide the best explanation as to the wide price gap between the two grades. It remains to the collector to decide if he wants to pony up nearly $20,000 for the superlative MS-66 speciman, or if he would be satisfied with the MS-65 for a fraction of the cost.

Notice the wide divergence in price among the retail price guides, from $1,880 to $3,850 for the MS-65. In this case, the $3,850 price may represent a coin graded with a "+" addendum or CAC certification. The *Blue Book* price is $1,275, and the *Grey Sheet* bid is $2,150 and ask is $2,300.

The NGC price is actually lower than the *Grey Sheet*, so we can throw it out — the possibility of finding a properly graded, retail priced coin 15 percent below the *Grey Sheet* does not seem realistic. It seems the effective price range for this coin in MS-65 is between $2,100 and $2,800, depending on how nice the coin is for the grade.

Photo courtesy Bart Crane

In MS-66, notice the PCGS price is far higher than the other three guides. For this reason, we should probably throw it out. Since the *Grey Sheet* ask is $16,500 — figuring for the dealer to make a profit — a likely market price for the coin is probably around $20,000. But it could vary up or down by a few percent.

While population reports can be useful, inherent deficiencies make it unwise to be a slave to population statistics. Just because a coin is rare does not guarantee it is a coin in demand. The 1922-S Peace dollar in MS-66 may be much rarer than the MS-65, but there might be a lack of buyers in the future for that coin, especially at that price. If a collector comes across a nice for the grade MS-65 he might experience a higher percentage return in the long run than he would on an MS-66. On the other hand, a lover of super high grade coins, especially if they like the *best known* category, may well jump at the chance to own a 1922-S in MS-66.

When searching for a particular coin, one can use this method for determining a coin's likely price range in advance of shopping. Still, one should remain aware that planning on paper does not account for the vagueries of the individual coins eventually considered. Nor does it take into account the personal traits and motivations of the seller. Negotiating the price of a coin is a lot like buying or selling a used car — it helps to have good debate and diplomacy skills, part of which is being able to read the guy on the other side of the table. Knowing a viable price range, though, will help get the negotiations started and will be the basis for formulating a bottom-line, walk-away number that represents a good value.

Chapter Six

Structuring Your Hard Asset Portfolio

BEFORE DISCUSSING THE STRUCTURE of a rare coin and precious metal hard asset portfolio and how to customize it to the individual's goals, we must define a few terms.

How is Numismatic Defined?

Numismatics is the study or collection of currency, including coins, tokens, paper money and related objects. Thus, anything relating to coins can be considered numismatic. For our purposes, however, numismatic coins are defined as those which, because of their collectability, are worth more than their face value.

For instance, any Lincoln cent minted 1958 or earlier — with the wheatback reverse — is numismatic by virtue of the fact that each one is now worth at least one and a half cents. A circulated 1984 Lincoln cent, meanwhile, is worth just one cent. Coins that are only worth face value are considered to be money, but not numismatic, because collectors do not pursue them. We call these coins *spendable* or *face-value* coins.

Types

The word *type* constantly shows up in numismatic literature. Probably the best translation of type when referring to coins is design. A good example of how denominations often have different types is the quarter, which has six different designs.

Two types of cents would be the Lincoln cent, and the Indian Head cent. Other types of U.S. cents include the Coronet Large, Braided Hair Large, and the Flying Eagle, among others.

The word type is also used in other ways when it comes to coins. One of the most common is the term *type set*. A type set contains one example of every type included.

The United States Mint has produced six different types of 25-cent coins from 1796 through the present: *(L to R)* Draped Bust quarter (1796-1807), Capped Bust quarter (1815-1838), Liberty Seated quarter (1838-1891), Barber quarter (1892-1916), Standing Liberty quarter (1916-1930), Washington quarter (1932-date). *Draped Bust, Capped Bust, Barber and Liberty Seated images courtesy Heritage Auctions (www.ha.com)*

Other examples of type sets would be a 20th-century type set, which contains one example of every type of coin issued by the U.S. from 1901 to 2000. A 20th-century gold type set would contain one example each of only the gold coins minted in that time frame. There is almost an endless number of type sets one can assemble.

Sometimes, the word type is confused with variety.

It is not uncommon for the U.S. Mint to make small design changes to a coin's basic type during certain years. These are called *varieties*.

Dealers and collectors commonly (mis-)use the word "type" when speaking about varieties.

A popular collector coin is the Buffalo nickel. The reverse of the 1913 Buffalo nickel comes in two varieties. Variety 1 shows what looks like raised ground on the reverse of the coin, right above where "five cents" appears. Variety 2 shows a straight line above the "five cents" on the reverse. Though it is more proper to call these Variety 1 and Variety 2, people often refer to these as Type 1 and Type 2 Buffalo nickels.

The same is true for the 1917 Standing Liberty quarter. Variety 1 shows no stars below the eagle on the reverse, and Variety 2 shows three stars below the eagle. The $20 Liberty gold has three varieties, which are often referred to as Type 1, Type 2 and Type 3, but are more accurately described as Variety 1, Variety 2 and Variety 3.

In the case of the $20 double eagle, Variety 1 was minted from 1848 to 1866 and is distinguished by having no motto on the reverse. The motto missing from Variety 1 is found on Variety 2 (1866-1876) above the eagle on the reverse. It is the motto still used on U.S. coins today: "In God We Trust." On Varieties 1 and 2, the denomination on the reverse is "Twenty D." Variety 3 (1877-1907) is distinguished by the denomination that instead reads "Twenty Dollars."

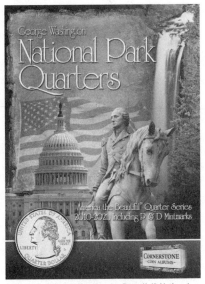

The U.S. Mint's "America the Beautiful" National Park quarters is a recent example of a popular program for series collectors.

Explanations and pictures of most of the major varieties can be found in the *Red Book*.

In contrast to the type collector is the *series* collector. In its purest form, the goal of a series collector is to obtain one example of a certain type coin from every year and every city where it was minted, including all major varieties. In other words, he will assemble a complete set of all dates and mintmarks of, say, Standing Liberty quarters. Some series collectors limit their sets to certain mintmarks. One of the most popular of these is comprised of the 13 dates of Morgan dollars minted in Carson City, a small subset of the entire Morgan series.

Key Date, Better Date and Common Date

Three other important terms frequently used to describe coins are: *key date, better date* and *common date.*

Key dates are far rarer, more difficult to find and have the highest numismatic premiums. Better dates are easier to find and less expensive. Common dates are the easiest to find because they exist in greater numbers and are consequently the least expensive of a series.

If we apply these terms to Morgan silver dollars, a key date would be the 1895 proof. While not rare compared to other proof issues of Morgan silver dollars (880 were minted as compared to as few as 500 for some other dates), it is the key date because no business

The 1893-S Morgan dollar has the lowest mintage business strike — less than 100,000 — of the entire series, which makes it a key date. An 1893-S Morgan in MS-67 (PCGS) sold for more than $1 million in 2008. Meanwhile, a comparable grade common date Morgan may change hands for less than $1,000.

strikes of the 1895 Morgan dollar were made at the Philadelphia Mint. To own an 1895 Morgan dollar with no mintmark, the only option is the 1895 proof — which makes it a key date. There are other key dates for Morgan dollars as well, such as the 1894, 1893-S and the 1889-CC.

Better dates for the Morgan dollar series would include all of the Carson City dollars, plus the 1888-S, 1894-S, 1895-S, 1893-O and 1899 to name a few. Common dates include the 1881-S, 1883-P, 1884-P and1885-P, 1883-O, 1884-O and 1885-O, among many others. An important distinguishing factor is that all common dates have similar prices for similar grades, from cull through MS-67.

For $20 St. Gaudens, the key date would be the 1907 High Relief, although some people put this coin in a category of its own. Non-high relief better dates include the 1920-S, 1921, 1926-D, 1927-S and 1929 to 1932. Some dates, like the 1909-D and 1911, are common in low grades, but are better dates in higher grades, whereas the 1924 and 1927 are common in all grades.

Structuring a Customized Precious Metals & Rare Coin Portfolio

After identifying your goals, needs and personal criteria, the next step requires making choices from the wide variety of rare coins and precious metals. To do so, it is useful to classify them into four groups: bullion, generic coins, rarities and low-value collectibles.

Gold and Silver Bullion

Bullion, whether gold or silver, is considered a safe-haven asset. Its main monetary uses are to store value, provide safety against a weakening dollar, and to use for trade in case of a catastrophic event. Of the hard asset classifications considered here, gold and silver bullion possess the minimum wild X factor in terms of their upward price potential since their value is not driven by collectors.

Although demand is the most powerful influence on the price of precious metals, the cost of production also plays a significant role. To illustrate the point, consider the 2012 average cost of production, which is approximately $1,300 per ounce for gold and $25 per ounce for silver.

While these figures might not indicate whether gold or silver will go up or down in the future, production costs provide insight for determining what constitutes good value in today's market. These prices suggest a minimal floor for precious metals because it is unlikely — though not impossible — for the market price to go below production cost for an extended period of time. Since the difference between today's prices and these production costs are small there appears to be little current downside potential for precious metals prices.

Still, gold and silver are traded through futures contracts and since those contracts are often subject to the same trading conditions as stocks (e.g., algorithm-driven computer trades, market panic, central bank buying and selling) precious metals prices can be subject to manipulation and volatility, especially in the short term.

Gold and silver bullion are considered to be the most conservative of these four hard asset classifications. They are much more liquid than numismatic assets, spreads between buy and sell prices are relatively narrow, and the over long term they have an excellent record of maintaining consistent value.

Generic Coins

Generic coins are U.S. coins made primarily of gold or silver. They are defined by several basic characteristics. First, they are common date. Second, they are uncirculated. Third, they are certified (only) by PCGS or NGC — because a fast moving liquid market requires that buys and sells be done on a sight unseen basis. Fourth, the coins must be favored enough to trade regularly.

When examining generic coins from the perspective of monetary instruments, it is useful to separate them into "gold" and "non-gold," which includes silver and nickel. Generally speaking, non-gold coins have relatively little bullion value compared to their overall value, whereas generic gold coins usually have a much greater value of bullion compared to total value.

Generic coins provide a useful compromise between rarities and bullion, deriving some value from their bullion content and some from their numismatic premium. As generic coins are all common date, the numismatic premium is based primarily on their grade.

Generics embody more of a wild X factor than bullion, but not as much as true rarities. The supply of generic coins is far greater than the supply of rarities, but far more limited than gold or silver bullion.

The percentage of a coin's value derived from the precious metals content versus numismatic premium varies from coin to coin, and grade to grade. The greater the percentage of value resulting from gold or silver content, the more it is impacted by fluctuations in gold and silver prices. The greater percentage of its value is determined by its numismatic premium, the more it will be influenced by collector-driven supply and demand dynamics of the individual coins involved.

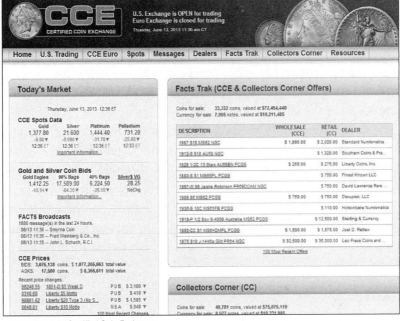

Image courtesy Certified Coin Exchange

Gold and non-gold generics traded on the Certified Coin Exchange:

Generic Gold	Grades	Generic Non-Gold	Grades
$20 St. Gaudens	MS-62 to MS-65	Morgan dollar	MS-63 to MS-67
$20 Liberty	MS-61 to MS-65	Peace dollar	MS-63 to MS-65
$10 Indian	MS-62 to MS-65	Walking Liberty half	MS-64 to MS-66
$10 Liberty	MS-62 to MS-65	Mercury dime	MS-65 to MS-67 (Full Bands)
$5 Liberty	MS-62 to MS-65	Buffalo nickel	MS-65 to MS-67 (Var. 2)

The balance of that percentage is important for structuring hard asset portfolios because the percentage of the portfolio in bullion versus numismatic coins impacts risk, liquidity and time frame among other considerations. Generics can act either as expensive bullion or inexpensive numismatics, making them exceptionally flexible instruments for hard asset portfolios.

At current price levels, about 50 percent of the value of MS-63 generic Morgan dollars is derived from bullion content. In MS-65, the bullion value is around 20 percent, and in MS-67 the bullion value is only about 5 percent. Although, in my opinion, MS-67 Morgan dollars should properly be considered numismatic rather than generic, the lower the grade, the more a Morgan's price will be influenced by fluctuations in the silver market.

The same holds true for MS-62, MS-63 and MS-64 $20 St. Gaudens gold, whose current bullion value is between 75 and 85 percent of their total value. For MS-65s the bullion value is about 65 percent, whereas MS-66s derive about 40 percent of their value from bullion content.

Spreads on generic coins are generally higher than bullion, but lower than true rarities. Because of the potential for increase in numismatic premiums, one of the best ways to hold gold is in the form of generic $20 gold coins.

Rarities

Rarities are coins whose value is primarily determined by their collectibility. As a monetary tool, they provide some safety and security, along with the ability to make a tremendous amount of value easily portable. They also have the highest wild X factor of all the hard asset classes, which means they have the greatest chance to appreciate far beyond their face value or precious metal content.

The history of rare coins has exhibited increases in value that are nothing short of miraculous. All one need do is observe the prices at which rare collectible coins now sell and compare them to the value of that coin at the time it was minted.

There are literally thousands of examples which bear this out. One is the 1916-D Mercury dime, with a silver content worth roughly $2 today, but because of its rarity, even a specimen in poor condition is worth at least $600 to $800. The 1895 proof Morgan dollar provides another example, with even low-grade, damaged specimens now worth more than $20,000.

According to PCGS, 235 individual coins have either sold for over one million dollars, or would sell for more than one million if they were placed at auction. A 1794 Flowing Hair silver dollar recently became the first coin to sell for over $10 million!

Hundreds if not thousands of others have sold in the six-figure range, and literally millions of coins have sold for over $1,000 apiece, despite the fact that the largest denomination of any coin ever produced by the U.S. Mint is only $50. Many coins minted since 1964 have also increased significantly beyond their face value, primarily because of being in superb condition, but in some cases because of rarity or rare variety. The extra leaf varieties of the 2004 Wisconsin state quarter are a perfect example.

Rarities carry unique risks. Price swings can be significant depending on whether they are in or out of favor with collectors. Sometimes there are few buyers for truly rare coins, and if one needs to sell quickly, the only offers might be much lower than desired. These risks are very much the same as for buyers of other high-end collectibles.

Rare coins also tend to have a higher spread between buy and sell prices than either bullion or generic coins. Despite their wild X factor, rare coins offer limited suitability for people who have no interest in collecting coins, or for those who are unwilling to approach the purchase of rare coins with a collector mentality — unless of course, they hire expert help.

Low-Value Collectibles

Although lacking the glamour, style and romance of high-grade certified rarities, *low-value* collectibles have also experienced significant price increases over the years. With few exceptions, every coin minted by the United States from the 1700s to 1964, from half-cent to $20 coins, is worth more as collectibles or in precious metal value than their face value.

1892 Barber (or Liberty Head) half dollar in XF-45 (NGC) sold for $246.75 at auction (Sept 2013). *Image courtesy Heritage Auctions (www.ha.com)*

Common date Large cents minted prior to 1856, which were made of copper, are worth around $10 even in very low grades, and roughly $50 in VF condition — approximately 500 times their original value. Indian Head cents in average circulated condition are worth a minimum of $.50 to $.75 each, and in just a little better condition, $1 or more — about 100 times their face value. Barber half dollars in G condition or worse are presently priced near their bullion content, about $8, but in XF condition are worth $150 to $250. (In gem condition, Barber halves go in the $5,000 to $15,000 range, and the key date 1904-S goes in the neighborhood of $30,000.)

Also included in this category are super high-grade coins that were recently minted, because they can be collected currently at close to face or bullion value, but may be rare enough in the future to command a healthy numismatic premium.

Many low-value collectors favor silver coins whose value is close to their silver content. While such coins are not generic as defined above, they possess some similar characteristics in that their value is split between precious metals content and their numismatic premium.

One of the attractive features of low-value collectibles is that they tend to have little downside over the long term, and sometimes experience exceptional upsides when measured on a percentage basis. Low-value rarities are typically the arena of the hobbyist. Low specimen prices make collecting coins accessible to almost everyone.

Hard Asset Portfolio Diversification

Diversification in a hard asset portfolio is a wise inclusion in a person's overall financial strategy. It provides flexibility when it comes time to sell, and increases the odds that at least some part of the portfolio will appreciate powerfully, regardless of future economic conditions. Diversification also protects against a serious drop in value for one classification or another.

Two money bags containing 500 Peace dollars each. *Photo courtesy Bart Crane*

An excellent way to structure diversification in a precious metals and rare coin hard asset portfolio is through simple percentages. Someone with a $100,000 portfolio may allocate 30 percent to gold bullion, 30 percent to silver bullion, 20 percent to generic gold and 20 percent to rarities. Exact percentages will vary from individual to individual.

Someone who is a collector, but is also concerned about the drop in the value of the dollar might take the same $100,000 and divide it into three equal parts of bullion, generics and rarities. Or, he might allocate $10,000 for silver, $25,000 for gold, $15,000 for generics, and $50,000 to assemble a type set of key date coins in high grade.

Diversification also works with smaller-sized portfolios, although this will tend to restrict choice. If one has $10,000 with which to work, he might eschew rarities and generics, and put $5,000 into bullion and $5,000 into low-value coins. Other collectors might put all their money into low-value coins, or into gold generics, because both of these have hybrid qualities that include both bullion and numismatic factors.

For those uncertain about what the future holds, the best policy is a balance between bullion, generics and rarities. Even collectors should probably own some gold and silver bullion, or at the very least, some generic coins. A person's choices will be affected by the length of time required to accumulate the portfolio as well as ongoing economic developments.

Another question one would be wise to explore when structuring a portfolio is: "When do I expect to sell?" A person's age and health are a part of this consideration. For lifelong collectors, this might not matter much. For a short-term hold, though, it is advisable to stick to bullion or generic gold, which are not only simpler and enjoy lower spreads, but are the most consistently liquid of all physically held hard assets. The same might apply if the accumulator is of advanced years, and he wants to hold some hard assets in case of financial upheaval.

If one is younger than 70, in good health and planning to divest from coins as needed during his retirement years, it is probably smart to lean more heavily toward generics and rarities. If less than 60 and looking for the long term, rarities almost certainly hold the greatest upside potential.

Chapter Seven

Rare Coins as an Investment

THE ABILITY OF RARE COINS TO APPRECIATE in value was well established long before rare coins were commonly considered an investment. In 1987, when the investment firm of Salomon Brothers (now part of Citigroup) issued their annual Investment Scorecard that rated the long- and short-term performance of various investments, the numbers were impressive.

The report found that rare coins had appreciated at a rate of 17 percent per year over a 15-year period — a higher rate of return than any other investment category. Setting aside the methodology that produced the report, which is problematic for several reasons, its publication in the *Wall Street Journal* created one of the most effective sales tools for people selling rare coins at that time.

Suddenly, rare coins were no longer the sole domain of collectors. Wall Street got involved. Investment firm Kidder Peabody established a rare coin fund structured somewhat similar to a standard mutual fund, consisting of rare coins instead of stocks. Investors poured millions of dollars into the market with gleeful abandon, clamoring to be part of the next golden opportunity.

The large influx of new cash from Wall Street increased demand for rare coins, which was further augmented by coin companies, some newly formed, that employed aggressive telemarketing techniques. These firms targeted new investors who were unfamiliar with the rare coin market, but purchased based on the profit potential presented to them via sales prospectuses. Prices soared.

Long before peak prices were reached in June of 1989, knowledgeable and experienced coin buyers had recognized a price bubble in the works and stopped buying. With sales evaporating and loaded with high-priced inventory, dealers would only buy at steep discounts — if at all.

To make matters worse, the economy went into recession. The FTC further squeezed the rare coin market by launching an investigation of the three-year-old Professional Coin Grading Service. This caused uncertainty for what was then the unproven concept of guaranteed certified grading, a critical lynchpin for transforming rare coins into an investment vehicle. Demand dropped and coin prices plummeted. The Kidder Peabody fund experienced losses so enormous that the firm refunded their investor's money to avoid a class-action lawsuit.

These negative factors sent the rare coin market into the doldrums for most of the 1990s. Even so, an important transition had occurred: Rare coins were now considered an investment and the label stuck. This enabled many in the rare coin business to appeal to the incorrect-but-familiar investor mindset of stock market thinking to sell coins.

On one level, it is completely understandable: Salespeople will use whatever tools available to make a sale. Speaking about coins as if they were stocks to people who are familiar with stocks was a powerful sales strategy. It also feels natural to refer to $20 St. Gaudens in MS-65, BU Morgan dollar rolls or bags of 90-percent silver just as if they were shares of GM, Apple or IBM. Furthermore, there is significant statistical data about coins that can be used to reinforce that idea, including original mintages, PCGS and NGC population reports and price charts.

None of this changed the fact that coins are collectibles. Thinking about them the same way one thinks about stocks is counterproductive and decreases the potential success of using rare coins effectively as monetary tools.

It cannot be proven statistically, but in purchasing coins from hundreds of people, along with experiences related by other dealers,

I've noted that the difference in results between collectors and investors is striking and overwhelming. Almost without exception, collectors are much happier with their results and profited to a much greater extent than self-described investors.

Between 1947 and 1971 Pablo Picasso created more than 3,000 ceramic objects at the Madoura Pottery factory. *Permission courtesy © 2013 Estate of Pablo Picasso / Artists Rights Society (ARS), New York*

My first experience with the monetary power of thinking like a collector turned out to be one of the best financial moves I ever made — approximately a 2,000-percent return. While in Cannes, France in 1975 for my junior year abroad, I happened upon an *atelier,* a studio that produced Picasso ceramics. I knew nothing about investments and precious little about art, but I clearly remember my thought process:

"These are beautiful. I love Picasso. He just died a couple of years ago — what a loss to humanity — but that means that no more of these ceramics will be produced. They will likely go up in price. In any case,

I doubt their value will fall. And even if they do, I won't care — they are so beautiful I will happily own them forever!"

The *atelier* exhibited a wide variety of ceramics, ranging in price from a little over $100 to many thousands of dollars. I could afford $1,000. I liked the idea of owning several pieces and selected four delightful vases and two equally dazzling plates.

Current auction prices indicate I might have done better monetarily had I spent the entire $1,000 on one piece. But I had an additional personal consideration. I grew up in San Francisco, and planned to live in California — earthquake country. If a serious earthquake occurred I reasoned that smaller, sturdier pieces would more likely survive, and having more pieces increased the chances of at least some surviving intact. It also gave me flexibility when the time came to sell. I satisfied my cash needs by selling five for $12,000 and was able to keep my favorite — which I still enjoy immensely to this day.

More than a demonstration of the importance of personal considerations, my experience with the Picasso ceramics has larger ramifications. A side effect of the pieces' aesthetic enjoyment was an entirely stress-free ownership of what came to be one of my most profitable investments. Had I been thinking like an investor, I would have wondered who might buy the ceramics and for how much. How long will I have to wait? Instead, they were a wonderful conversation piece for many years, and the remaining plate still brightens my living room.

Accumulating Value

Rather than trying to find the "hottest deal" in the market, a collector with an eye to appreciation would determine if he actually wanted a certain coin in his vault 20 years from now. He would use statistical information mainly to assure that he was getting good value, which is always an important consideration.

As this method is geared toward accumulating value, it may well be called the "rich man's approach." Certainly this method is used by many people who are considered rich, but one need not be in order to employ it. Accumulating assets of value occurs on all levels of the economic ladder. It is a strategy that almost always improves one's station. It is a close cousin to value investing, in which one looks for desirable assets that are undervalued, and buys expecting they will become properly valued at some point in the future. The name of the game is increasing the quality and quantity of assets owned over time.

There is often a strong streak of contrarian thinking imbued in this mind set. The contrarian feels no need to be in lockstep with what is currently popular, or how others might judge his choices. Indeed, they may seek out what is unpopular at the moment due to the cyclical nature of such items.

This is not a hard and fast rule, however. Collectors will sometimes buy what is in demand, and refuse what is not in demand. If the accumulator wants to own a certain asset, he may even buy at non-ideal prices. If he does not want a certain asset, he will rarely buy it no matter how attractive the price. Investors, meanwhile, are more likely to search primarily for a bargain and focus less on the importance of owning a certain asset.

The Long-Term Approach

The value of long-term thinking cannot be overstated. First, trading for the short term requires more work and more time to do effectively. Also, because there is a higher cost to physical trading, overcoming that expense is much easier over the long term than the short term. The longer an asset is held and the higher the price goes, the less significant that cost becomes, because it is amortized over time. A 10-percent cost amortized over 10 years comes to 1 percent annually. With coins the spreads are much larger than with bullion, so accumulating for the long term is even more important with rarities than with bullion.

Focusing on long-term appreciation enables accumulators to all but ignore short-term fluctuations. If one believes silver will go to $100 an ounce within 10 years, whether he pays $19.50 or $21 per ounce is of little consequence. If silver does not reach $100 in 10 years, the long-term accumulator still owns an asset that will have value.

Accumulating for the long term also encourages collector thinking, because, in effect, an accumulator is a collector — a collector of assets. The long-term accumulator will therefore tend to spend more time focusing on what he wants to own rather than how much it will be worth in the future.

Foresight

Foresight involves looking at the big picture today, considering changes that might be afoot and imagining how circumstances will be ten or twenty years from now. Naturally, no one can predict the future precisely, but a general sense of where things are likely to go can be instructive. Even if one is wrong in some respects, he will likely be right in others.

We have already explored at some length how excessive money printing and a tenuous economic policy might affect the value of the dollar. Foresight provides the basis to get a handle of where the value of the dollar might be twenty years from now, and how that might affect precious metals and rare coin prices.

Foresight is also useful for considering what impact the diminishing use of cash might have on those markets. This began with the invention of the bank check, expanded with increasing use of credit and debit cards, and continues with the pervasive use of bar codes on smart phones and other portable devices. An increasing number of young people today do not use cash at all. Following that pattern, only a small percentage of money created by the Federal Reserve is actually printed in the form of paper currency, existing instead as electronic entries.

The trend will likely continue and could lead to a cashless society. Moreover, some have advocated discontinuing one-cent coins, because the cost of production exceeds the value of the coin itself. It's already happened in Canada. Will it happen in the U.S. too?

Foresight enables us to infer that certain coins will become increasingly rare and possibly obsolete in regular usage, which bodes well for those coins' collectibility factor.

Could society stop using coins? Forget about them entirely? I doubt it. Regardless of technology, human nature remains what it is. People will always want to hold tradable value physically in their hands. They will continue to appreciate the art, beauty and individuality as well as the gold and silver content of coins.

Another factor that could powerfully influence the value of rare coins is that population and prosperity are increasing worldwide, which should increase the number of collectors and the amounts they accumulate. We have already seen this with Chinese coins — the demand for which has greatly intensified in concert with the growth of a prosperous middle class. In India, a rapidly growing economy has also spurred the growth of coin collecting as a hobby.

In addition to political, economic and cultural issues, part of foresight involves personal considerations. "When I'm 75, I won't want to deal with volumes of heavy material — so I'd rather have gold or rare coins than silver because they are easier to physically manage," or, "After I retire, I want the security of having lots of silver eagles so that I can easily trade them for whatever I might need."

There are about 2,000 years of Chinese "cash" coinage available to collectors who favor the World & Ancient area of numismatics. Increased demand has caused prices to rise sharply in recent years. *Image of 1982 People's Republic of China gold Panda 100 yuan (1 oz.) courtesy Heritage Auctions (www.ha.com)*

Then there is that most intangible quality of taste. If the collector enjoys Morgan silver dollars, he buys them. If he likes Flying Eagle cents, Buffalo nickels and Mercury dimes he buys those particular types.

The collector mentality focuses on buying coins that fit his aesthetic considerations — design and grade — and his pocket book. The one other critical point is that he does not pay more than a competitive price for any of it. Furthermore, what one collector likes now will likely be desired by another collector in the future. In other words, the collector approach anticipates future collector demand.

It does not seem to matter what the collector collects, be it low-value coins or high-value rarities. What does matter is that the collector focus on the specific coin he is buying, then consider the price and the current value to determine what kind of deal should be made.

The investor on the other hand does not focus on the coin itself, and generally doesn't care whether he likes it or wants to own it in the future. He spends an inordinate amount of thought and energy trying to nab a coin at a short-term price dip. He is also susceptible to such fictions that one particular grade is ideal regardless of the coin. His decision-making process is muddied by a penny-wise/pound-foolish mentality.

The investor has expectations about the future price performance of coins, and worse yet, makes the mistake of basing a coin's future price performance on its past record of appreciation, or by examining price charts to outsmart the market. He may as well be reading tea leaves.

The collector's approach is completely antithetical to that of the investor. When a collector buys a coin, he may have an idea about how he will sell it, but he rarely creates expectations about when he is going to sell it or for how much. He might sell eventually for a variety of reasons, but he usually does not buy with an eye to selling it. He buys to own it.

Instead of resisting the unpredictability of market psychology and individual tastes, the collector accepts and embraces them. Instead of using investment-oriented mathematics to analyze future profit potential, he uses market knowledge to establish a coin's value in the realm of his own psychology and tastes. Instead of buying based on statistics, he focuses on whether or not the coin in question is the best choice for his portfolio of assets. This approach enhances one's ability to effectively harness the market's unpredictable and mercurial forces to his advantage.

Chapter Eight

Buying for Value

WHEN IT COMES TO COLLECTING COINS with an eye toward making a profit, there is no guaranteed formula. Rare coins appreciate due to collector demand, and the best way to tap into the process is to think like a collector.

Harnessing Your Intuition

Collectors are emotional about coins. Something draws them toward one type of coin or another. Therefore, the first step is to develop a collector's appreciation: What coins attract you? Fortunately, this is easily accomplished. It is no different than going to a museum. After all, rare coins are pieces of art. How can one learn to appreciate art if one does not take the time to experience it? Investors rarely do this; experienced collectors live by it.

Attending coin shows is an excellent method for improving one's critical evaluation and appreciation of numismatics. They provide a venue where one can view a wide variety. Spend a few hours walking around and looking at the specimens on display. See what coins catch the eye and entice second, third and fourth looks. Examine such coins closely and engage dealers in conversation about them. Sooner or later, at least one type of coin — and probably more than one — will emerge as a favorite. While this is essential for beginners, it is also useful for the experienced collector and for dealers. In 1999, when I was in a something of a rut, I spent a few hours wandering around a coin show with no purpose beyond enjoyment. It changed my perspective and opened up new possibilities for the direction of my coin business.

From a financial perspective, it doesn't really matter what kind of coin one chooses, from Morgan dollars to Lincoln cents, from $20 gold to proof Seated-type coins. There are opportunities — and outstanding appreciation is possible — with practically every type of coin or set of coins a collector might devise. What truly is important is making a choice and getting started.

For the new collector that means buying at least one coin. Don't be impatient and buy any coin just to buy a coin. Select a coin type you like, and choose an affordable grade for that coin that also appeals to your aesthetic taste. Buy for value. Focusing on only one coin type is simpler because it requires market knowledge only about that specific type. The investor is now a collector, or at the very least, an investor who now approaches coins like a collector.

Don't worry whether or not the coin you buy is exactly the right coin or the best choice. Work intuitively. You can buy a coin of one type and then choose another completely different type for your next purchase. Mistakes might be made, but if the methods outlined in this book are followed, they won't be devastating mistakes. Remember, any coin purchased becomes an asset, and from a financial perspective, the name of the game is accumulating assets. Have a good time with the process — coin collecting is supposed to be fun.

Financial Planning for Collectors

Regardless of whether one chooses to collect a series, a type set or any other kind of organized grouping, funds will be limited. Therefore, to collect a certain set or accumulation, it's better to budget in advance. Many collectors manage their funds by setting a per coin limit, per year limit, or by allocating a certain amount to a specific type and stopping when the money runs out.

Because the grade of the coin so strongly impacts the price, the collector can satisfy both his collecting desires and his financial goals by choosing sets that satisfy both grade level and price. The methodology is simple: Use a mainstream price sheet like the *Red Book, Coin World* Trends, or the PCGS or NGC online price guides to make a spreadsheet listing the coin type, date, grade and projected prices.

Not long ago, a collector developed just such a spread sheet for a series set of gem condition Peace dollars listing current purchase prices for all 24 dates in grades MS-64, MS-65 and MS-66.

He could easily afford the MS-64 set. The MS-66 set was far beyond his financial ability. The MS-65 set was also too expensive, primarily because of five dates: 1923-S, 1924-S, 1925-S, 1927-S and 1928-S. Prices for these coins were far higher in MS-65 than they were in MS-64. A few calculations revealed that if he bought these five coins in MS-64, he could afford to collect the rest of the set in MS-65.

His plan was complete. Knowing the target grade for each date freed him to focus his energies toward comparing actual coins and prices to obtain the best value. In all likelihood, his set will sell for a great deal more in 20 years than he paid originally, particularly if assembled with good aesthetics. Even if prices do not rise as hoped, he will have an excellent collection of gem condition Peace silver dollars — a wonderful savings account.

					Peace Dollar Collector Sheet				
					Current (10/2013) Retail Prices				
Year	Target Grade	Grade Obtained	P/N	Price Paid	MS-63	MS-64	MS-65	MS-66	Notes
1921	MS-65				$500	*$1,100*	*$2,700*	$8,500	
1922	MS-65				$40	$60	*$200*	$700	
1922-D	MS-65				$55	$125	*$450*	$2,300	
1922-S	MS-65				$85	*$425*	$2,500	$14,000	
1923	MS-65				$40	$60	*$200*	$700	
1923-D	MS-65				$140	*$340*	*$1,300*	$6,000	
1923-S	MS-64				$75	*$450*	$6,500	$15,000	
1924	MS-65				$40	$60	*$225*	$700	
1924-S	MS-64				$700	*$1,700*	$10,000	$50,000	
1925	MS-65				$40	$60	*$200*	$700	
1925-S	MS-64				$200	*$700*	$22,000	$30,000	
1926	MS-65				$85	$125	*$450*	$2,000	
1926-D	MS-65				$150	$300	*$700*	$2,200	
1926-S	MS-65				$100	*$275*	*$1,000*	$6,000	
1927	MS-65				$175	*$350*	$2,700	$22,000	
1927-D	MS-65				$350	*$900*	$5,500	$25,000	
1927-S	MS-64				$450	*$1,700*	$14,000	$45,000	
1928	MS-65				$900	*$1,500*	$5,000	$15,000	
1928-S	MS-64				$700	*$1,800*	$23,000	$35,000	
1934	MS-65				$275	$500	*$900*	$4,000	
1934-D	MS-65				$400	$700	$2,000	$5,000	
1934-S	MS-65				*$4,500*	$6,000	*$8,500*	$22,000	
1935	MS-65				$110	*$225*	*$700*	$2,200	
1935-S	MS-65				$450	*$700*	*$1,600*	$3,000	

While setting limits is an excellent and useful strategy, it is also a good idea to recognize that these limits will not always correspond perfectly with market pricing and opportunity. Our Peace dollar collector might come across a 1925-S Peace dollar in MS-64 that is of superlative quality, perhaps with a "+" grade or a CAC sticker. The extra cost for such a coin might put him over his pre-set limit, but if the coin represents the best value for that date, or if his collector's desire is strong enough, it probably makes financial sense to break his own limit. This is especially true for superlative key or rare dates, because they have greater X factor potential for extraordinary financial gain over time. That's why it is a good idea to allow for some leeway when budgeting.

Eye Appeal

Always buy pretty coins and avoid ugly ones. As pointed out in Chapter 4 on grading, eye appeal refers to the coin's beauty, which is different than the technical grade of the coin. Even so, eye appeal affects the value of coins, sometimes significantly. Aesthetics are very important for the value-oriented buyer, and it is precisely this kind of collector who will likely receive the highest price for his coins in the future.

Most issues of eye appeal, including toning, uneven wear and poorly placed marks were covered in Chapter 4. One not covered there is copper spotting. Like other aesthetic values, copper spotting does not affect the technical grade of the coin, but does affect value. Spotting on copper coins is easy to see, due to obvious corrosion. They are also easy to see on silver because their dark tone stands in stark contrast with the bright silver of the rest of the coin. With gold coins, however, copper spots frequently blend into the coin's yellow, orange and gold hues and escape detection from a cursory glance. Be sure to carefully examine all gold coins with a quality loupe for copper spots as they can reduce value by as much as 10 to 15 percent — or more if the spotting is severe.

One of the big problems with copper spotting is that once the spot has started, it tends to increase in size and intensity over time, even if encased in PCGS or NGC holders, or other inert plastic. Intense spotting can develop into corrosion, which, once established, only gets worse. Corrosion is characterized by greenish spots with a rust-like texture. Coins with corrosion are to be avoided, as it drastically lowers or completely destroys a coin's numismatic value. PCGS and NGC will not certify corroded coins. This is another reason to purchase only coins which are certified by PCGS or NGC, and why corrosion is more of a problem for uncertified coins.

Another aesthetic consideration is the *strike*, which refers to the depth and crispness of the design. Stronger strikes are more desirable, but the price differences are less significant unless the strike is unusually poor. Strike characteristics are different for each type of coins and easier to recognize by comparing examples side by side.

Grade and Price Differentials – Buying for Value

Higher grades tend to appreciate more than lower grades of the same coin, especially over the long term. Obtaining higher grades for relatively small additional numismatic premiums makes sense from a value standpoint.

This leads us to examine one of the most common mantras about how to buy rare coins. In various forms, it states: "Buy the highest grade coin one can afford." Despite the tendency of higher grade coins to appreciate faster, high grade alone does not assure a faster or greater percentage increase in price than lower grade coins of the same date and type. At any given time, coins in lower grades might present better value — in terms of percentage — than coins of higher grade.

The way collectors and smart investors consider this issue is by paying attention to the price difference between grades: Is the higher grade coin worth the extra cost? Let's examine the 1924 $20 St. Gaudens, the most common date of the series.

VF	XF	AU	MS-60	MS-62	MS-63	MS-64	MS-65	MS-66	MS-67	MS-68
$1,575	$1,610	$1,640	$1,720	$1,900	$2,050	$2,200	$2,600	$3,300	$13,000	$45,000

*Note: Prices in this chart are approximate, designed to illustrate the concept and will be different than actual current prices.

Despite the huge difference in quality between VF and MS-63, the price differential is minimal. Unless accumulating solely for gold value, almost all collectors would and should pay the little extra for an MS-63 over a VF and lower grades. Prices increase gradually from grades MS-63 through MS-66 and then take a sudden, large leap at MS-67. It is easy to see that a strong case can be made for buying an MS-64 instead of an MS-63. The additional premium is relatively small.

An equally strong case can also be made for buying an MS-65 over an MS-64. By comparing the quality difference between MS-64 and MS-65 and taking into account the population differences, the collector can get a sense of which grade provides the best value. While considering if an MS-66 is preferable to MS-65 — in which the price differential is larger — the buyer will have to pay some attention to the value of gold versus the numismatic value and its relationship to his goals when making that choice.

The issue becomes more ambiguous when considering an MS-66 versus MS-67. The reason for this is that the price break between these two grades is abruptly huge, around $10,000. The relative population between the two partially explains the difference, as the number of MS-67s is a fraction of the MS-66 population.

But the question remains: Is the additional $10,000 worth obtaining the coin in the higher grade? Financial limits might answer this if the $13,000 is out of range for the collector. If $13,000 is within financial range, however, the collector must determine if the quality difference is worth the money. He could also compromise with a "+" or CAC MS-66, which, depending on price and the aesthetics of the individual coin might be a better value. In the end, he may determine that the quality is so important and the MS-67 population so low that the additional premium is worth it. This is where means, intuition and tastes of the individual collector play a powerful role.

Alternatively, our collector might think: "I already have an MS-65 St. Gaudens that I love, so maybe I should get an MS-65 $20 Liberty instead." Notice that the concept of diversification is built into collector thinking. It's part of a collector's DNA. He would then go through the same process of value determination with the $20 Liberty. If the current value seems greater with the $20 Liberty than with the St. Gaudens, the collector would do well to make that choice.

The collector looks for the grade where the price breaks, in other words, right before there is a sizable jump in price, and then makes his choice in terms of obtaining the best value for his money. This is what ties him into the collector mentality, which is the foundation of buying for value. In the case of the 1924 St. Gaudens, regardless of whether he chooses an MS-66 or MS-67, the collector will not become impatient if the price doesn't move quickly. He is in it for the long term, for the enjoyment, and to accumulate assets.

Market Timing

The term itself implies that when someone buys or sells is the key to profitability. While this is sometimes true when large price swings occur in a short period of time, what really creates good market timing is buying for value.

The 1804 Idler/Bebee Draped Bust dollar, dubbed the "King of U.S. Coins." If you have to ask, you haven't got enough. Still, a collector can dream! *Image courtesy ANA Money Museum*

Recently, a client expressed a desire to buy MS-66 Walking Liberty half dollars. They were coins he liked. They had recently been selling at around $300, but he had been following price levels and believed they might be available for under $200. He was right and made a purchase.

How this will turn out remains to be seen. There is no concrete evidence he can point to that indicates a price increase for these particular coins is imminent. For him, it was a good value purchase. He obtained the coins he desired while also accumulating an asset he figures has excellent upside potential in the long term.

Market timing for coins often has much to do with availability. For example, an 1893-S Morgan dollar in AU condition is rare, one of the key dates of the series. Finding an AU example might be tough, but eventually one will become available, especially if the collector is flexible about the grade. On the other hand, if the collector specifically wants one that is PCGS AU-55, blast white, with superbly struck chest feathers, he might have to wait an extraordinarily long time for a such a speciman to surface. It could be he never obtains one.

If an 1893-S in AU condition is the target, should the buyer hold out for the perfect example? Perhaps. But it probably makes more sense to purchase the first decent coin he can get at good value. If his dream coin comes along later, he can always buy it as well. There is little financial downside to having two examples of a key and in-demand rarity. Since the coin is fairly expensive in AU, ranging from $20,000 to $50,000, the collector can always sell the less desirable speciman if that makes financial sense.

A perfect 1893-S might become available, but at a price higher than ideal. Whether this is a good value or not is subjective — it depends on how strong is the collector's desire to own that coin, and also whether the high price corresponds to the superlative quality of the coin. While rarity and price sheets provide indicators, they are not perfect. There are no set rules as to how much above the price sheet one should pay for a superlative example. The collector must make a judgment call.

Considerations Specific to Modern Coins

Sometimes the U.S. Mint creates a limited edition for which demand exceeds supply. This happened with the 25th Anniversary Silver Eagle Set, which went from its issue price of around $300 to over $1,000 within weeks of release. It also happened with the 2009 Ultra High

Relief $50 gold, whose initial U.S. Mint price was $1,189 and now sells above $2,500. But beware, there is also a risk that new releases will initially soar in price only to fall just as suddenly if collector demand does not hold over time. Thus, if one believes that an upcoming Mint issue is likely to experience extraordinary demand, especially if it is a low-mintage edition, it makes sense to place an order with the Mint as soon as possible, rather than wait for the coin to rise and then buy.

Predicting Future Demand

Collector demand is unpredictable. That said, what collectors like today, other collectors are likely to prefer in the future, and collector demand for a coin that is inherently rare or attractive creates upward pressure on prices over time. This occurs most frequently with high eye appeal key and better dates, the kind series collectors must acquire to complete their sets. This is one reason collectors frequently focus on them, and thus, it is also an outstanding investment-oriented strategy.

The goal is to buy for value, accumulate for the long term and approach your dealings with a collector mentality. Focus on specific types, quality and aesthetics, key and rare dates, and higher grades. Pay attention to grade price differentials and avoid the pitfalls covered in Chapter 10. Utilize market information, but do not be enslaved by the investor mentality.

Chapter Nine
Inheritance

THE IDEA OF ACCUMULATING ASSETS for one's children or grandchildren is powerfully attractive — we want our heirs to be protected and secure. These assets will be a source of empowerment, enjoyment and wealth, a family legacy to be passed from generation to generation and, of course, a life-saving nest egg in case of an emergency.

Recently, a gentleman sent for valuation a collection he had enjoyed helping his father assemble, and which had been passed down to him. He was now in his 80s, was no longer accumulating and was thinking of selling. The coins were pulled out of change, nothing extraordinary, but they had appreciated in value over time and he was delighted with the offer. When he told his daughter and only heir about the coins, he was surprised to find she had recently acquired an interest in numismatics. He told me that passing the coins to his daughter was like bringing his efforts and those of his father full circle.

Not all inheritances are so simple. Sometimes heirs have no interest in coins, or don't get along. Some collections might also contain a wide assortment of obscure items, difficult for the novice to research and sell.

In such cases, liquidating a collection before inheritance becomes an issue is often the best course of action. Not only will the collector likely get more for his coins, but it saves the heirs from what can be a time consuming and difficult task at an emotionally challenging time, and eliminates an asset that could be an issue of contention among the heirs.

Important Precautions

Keep an up to date list of where coins are located. This ensures that the entire collection actually makes its way into possession of the heirs, and that no coins are lost or misplaced. Keep an inventory including prices paid and from whom they were purchased. Leave notes with specific information about any particularly valuable or unusual items. Include contact information for dealers or other collectors with whom one has had a good relationship. The advice of knowledgeable and reputable people is a tremendously valuable resource: Heirs almost always feel more comfortable dealing with someone who had known and worked with their parents.

Collectors who intend to pass on their accumulations should educate their heirs. No additional planning may be necessary if the heirs are already collectors and prepared to take over the stewardship of the collection the same way one might take over a family farm or business. If there is more than one heir, and especially if one or more plan to keep their share of the collection while others are likely to sell, it often makes sense to divide the collection in advance.

A variation of this solution is to make the collection easy to divide among the heirs. This is most effectively accomplished if the legacy consists of multiples of similar bullion, generic and rare coins. If there are three heirs, the collector might plan to have three of everything, or quantities that can be divided equally by three. Thus, he might have three $20 Liberty gold coins in MS-64, nine St. Gaudens in MS-65, 300 ounces of silver, 18 common date MS-65 Morgan dollars, three proof sets for every year for which he has proof sets, and so forth.

Including bullion and generic gold as a significant part of any legacy is an excellent strategy because information about them and their values is accessible even for the non-expert. They are also widely and frequently traded, so they are relatively easy to sell and prices offered will likely be competitive.

The most important part of planning a legacy is designing it to fit the heirs. This principle will powerfully inform as to what preparations to make and what coins to include. The kinds of coins best suited for a legacy portfolio would comprise a mix of bullion, generic coins, and PCGS/NGC certified rarities. In other words, a legacy portfolio looks a great deal like any portfolio a collector might assemble for himself, but with more emphasis on the needs, abilities and situation of the inheritors. Take into account their coin knowledge and interest, the number of heirs, the length of time they are likely to retain possession, the specific purpose of the legacy if applicable, plus personal considerations.

Rare Coin Inheritance

Receiving an inheritance of precious metals and rare coins is a wonderful gift. One can keep it as a legacy for passing down to one's own heirs, in which case the only action to take is to assure safe storage. One can also continue the accumulation process by being (or becoming) a collector and buying more hard assets. Another option is to donate the collection to a 501(c)(3) non-profit organization and take a tax deduction. In this case, a formal appraisal is necessary.

The other option is to sell. This is the option that raises anxiety for most people, especially if they are new to coins. The problem usually lies in the fear that they will not get fair value for their coins, or that someone will rip them off. It is a valid concern. How does a novice make sure that they will get fair value? Because there are so many kinds and forms of precious metals and rare coins, the question appears to boil down to the following: either learn enough to become an expert, or trust someone who is an expert. A good book on the subject is *What to do with Granddaddy's Coins* (Zyrus Press) by Jeff Ambio.

The problem with becoming an expert is that it cannot be accomplished overnight. The amount of information is too vast, too great a commitment for most people to learn. Even then, buying and selling coins is not always an easy process. The time and energy necessary to find buyers at desirable price levels for what one has to sell can be prohibitive for the non-professional.

Many people choose to trust a dealer. If they choose well, they will be rewarded with a good price for their collection. But if they choose poorly, they will not. Take some time to research, meet and speak with dealers until you are satisfied you have found the right one for you (see Chapter 13).

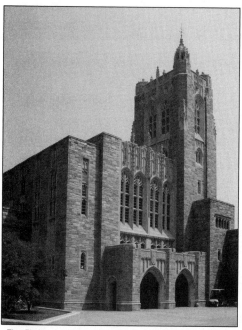

The Firestone Library, home to the Princeton University numismatic collection, houses more than 60,000 specimens, many of which were bequeathed by alumi. *Photo courtesy of the Numismatic Collection, Department of Rare Books and Special Collections, Firestone Library, Princeton University*

Do not remove coins from albums or from packaging. In some cases, a coin's value is enhanced because of the packaging. Do not clean or wash coins in any way whatsoever — it can destroy numismatic value, potentially costing thousands of dollars.

If one has already found a trusted dealer, or doesn't mind leaving some money on the table, he might choose to avoid the sorting part of the inventory process. For someone who is looking for a dealer, an inventory sheet is an expedient way to narrow the field.

Sort the collection before creating a written inventory. This crucial step saves a great deal of time and energy. Have a *Red Book* handy for reference. Assemble the entire collection in one place, then group similar items in boxes and zip-lock bags according to the traditional classifications below:

- Certified coins in sealed plastic slabs: Place in order of denomination and date.

- Precious metals bullion: Separate by metal (gold, silver, platinum, etc.) and type.
- Raw coins that are loose, in rolls, cardboard holders or albums: Separate by denomination and type. Treat 40-percent silver coins (half dollars 1965-1970) and clad coinage (half dollars 1971 and later, quarters and dimes 1965 and later) as separate types.
- Proof sets: Put in order of date.
- Mint sets: Put in order of date.
- Commemorative coins: Group similar together.
- Banknotes and currency: Large-size U.S. notes can be quite valuable, and any U.S. banknote that looks unusual will likely have some value beyond its face value, especially if in excellent condition. Separate these from non-U.S. banknotes, most of which will likely be of limited value.
- World coins: Most modern (after 1970) world coins have nominal value unless they contain silver or gold. Pay special attention to any coins that appear to be made of gold or silver, or ancient coins that appear to be of Roman, Greek or Byzantine origin.
- Miscellaneous: This applies to anything that does not fit the above classifications and for items you cannot identify. Sometimes people take a handful of such items to a coin show to get a dealer's thoughts, which is not a bad idea.

Once the sorting is complete, use a *Red Book* or other price sheet to help identify and notate the key dates of each type. Price sheets will show these as being worth far more than their common-date counterparts. Having this knowledge before entering into any transaction negotiation is one of the best ways to assure good value when selling. If desired, one can obtain a more detailed cash valuation estimate of key dates by using the *Red Book* and *Blue Book* together as described in Chapter 5 on Pricing.

If there is a large quantity of bulk coinage, such as a five-gallon water bottle filled with Lincoln cents, there is a time-versus-money consideration. Is taking the time and energy of going through all those coins worth the extra money if a couple of key dates are found? Frequently it will not be. That said, you never know. In any event, it's a judgement call you'll have to make.

Now compile an inventory sheet. List all certified coins individually. Duplicate coins of the same denomination, date, type and grade (e.g., five 1881-S Morgan dollars in MS-65) can be listed on one line. Do the same for key dates, and mint and proof sets. Bullion and bulk coins need only be counted. While this sounds like a lot to do, the fact is that except for exceptionally large and complex collections, this process should only take a few hours at most, even for a novice, and it is almost always time well spent.

Do not sell to pawn shops. They usually pay the least for any collection, first, because offering pennies on the dollar is their business model and, second, because the proprietors are rarely coin experts and won't be willing to pay strong prices for something of which they're not 100 percent sure. Travelling buying events usually operate like pawn shops and also should be avoided.

It is not a good idea to take your accumulation with you in the beginning, not even to coin shows. Instead, create an inventory list. Show it to dealers and use the ensuing discussion to see how the dealer approaches making a purchase. Talk with more than one dealer, whether by telephone or in person at a coin show or at a shop. Ask questions about the coins. Get ballpark price estimates. Ask more questions if necessary. These conversations will be revealing, and, in most cases, the right dealer will become apparent.

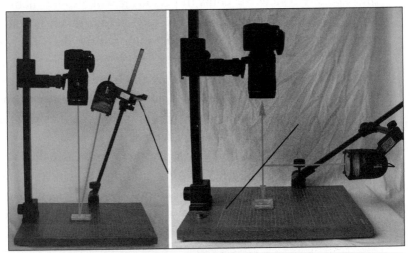

Numismatic photography lighting techniques. *Photos courtesy Mark Goodman*

If the collection is exceptionally valuable, particularly if consisting mainly of high-end certified coins, and if no one dealer surfaces as preferred, it might make sense to let more than one dealer bid on the collection. If doing so, let the bidding dealers know in advance. When offering the collection out to bid, it is best to limit the bidding to two and never more than three dealers, which is sufficient competition to get the best price.

Another method, especially useful for larger, more valuable accumulations, or when the collection is part of a formal inheritance, is to use a professional appraisal. Be sure to get a quote in advance of services being rendered. A professional appraisal is different than an offer to purchase. Appraisals are used to establish insurance value, or replacement value, which are typically much higher than appraisals for cash value. Be clear about what kind of appraisal you are requesting. Once the appraisal is done, it is time to get offers.

The advantage of this method is that competing dealers can be given a copy of the appraisal, saving them a great deal of time when they actually review the coins in person. It will also let them know if it is a collection they truly want to buy — remember, not all dealers are right for all coins. Perhaps, most importantly, the seller will have benchmarks to be reassured that he is getting good value. Also, because appraisal services are usually billed by the hour, a seller can use some of that time to ask any questions not yet answered. Frequently, the appraiser will want to make an offer, and sometimes they will rebate all or part of their fee if their bid is accepted.

If one has super valuable coins, another option is selling the coins at auction. There are numerous issues and pitfalls with this approach, ranging from choosing an auction company and choosing a time and place to negotiating auction fees and conditions. If considering this option, it is a good idea to hire a dealer as a consultant.

Chapter Ten

Avoiding the Pitfalls

FROM TIME TO TIME — FAR TOO OFTEN for my taste — I have heard heart-breaking stories of people who have lost a great deal of money through buying rare coins and precious metals. While some of these were the result of buying coins at the height of the 1989 rare coin bubble, the vast majority were for matters unrelated to market pricing. Rather, they were the result of easily avoidable mistakes made by people who were unaware of the potential dangers. Helping people to avoid these pitfalls is one of the main goals of this book.

Pitfall #1: Improperly Graded Coins & Uncertified (or Raw) Coins

Learning how to grade coins properly requires knowledge, skill and practice. It is also the best protection against buying improperly graded uncertified coins. It is essential for buyers of raw coins to learn these skills, as various problems, some difficult to recognize, can eviscerate a coin's value. These include cleaning, rim nicks, tooling, whizzing, gashes, graffiti, artificial color, polishing, mintmark alteration and counterfeiting.

There are books — *Photograde* by James Ruddy (Zyrus Press) and *ANA Grading Standards* by Ken Bressett and Q. David Bowers (Whitman) are two good ones — and many online guides that provide an excellent education about grading, including the ways different types and varieties show wear. Academic study while valuable is no substitute for practice and the guidance from experienced graders, dealers and savvy collectors one might meet at coin clubs, coin shows or online.

If just starting with coins, it is best to concentrate on learning to grade one type. After you're proficient grading one type, select another and practice with that one. The more types learned, the faster your grading skills will develop, until eventually you'll become a decent grader for almost any type. Mistakes may be made, but by starting with inexpensive coins they won't be costly and the education gained will prove to be immensely useful in the future. Sifting through raw coins looking for bargain buys is a favorite pastime of most collectors. Good grading skills will vastly improve your chances of spotting an undiscovered gem.

Certified Coins

Buying PCGS- and NGC-graded coins eliminates most, though not all, of the monetary risks associated with poor grading. It helps protect novice buyers from unscrupulous sellers.

An inadvertent benefit of professionally graded coins is providing benchmarks for you to practice your own grading skills. While the grades awarded do not reveal the specifics of why a coin was scored at a certain level, comparing and examining certified coins will give you insight that will improve your grading skills.

Pitfall #2: Misuse of Population Reports

In their early years, before they certified many coins, PCGS and NGC population reports often indicated that coins were far rarer than they really were. Unscrupulous sellers would often victimize new buyers by using inaccurate numbers to justify highly inflated prices. More than 25 years later, with tens of millions of coins certified, their population reports are more useful, but still far from perfect.

These reports do not account for coins never submitted. For some types and dates, that number can be huge. Be especially wary if the rarity offered is a modern coin with a large mintage figure, but even older dates and types can have many coins not yet certified.

As time goes on, more coins will be graded, and population figures will increase for almost all coins.

On the flip side, coins submitted again and again to both services in an attempt to get the highest grade can show inflated population figures in the reports, especially when large price spreads between adjoining grades are concerned.

PCGS grading room where three numismatists independently examine coins and then caucus to reach a concensus on the final grade, circa late-1980s. *Photo courtesy PCGS*

One final point: Rarity alone does not determine the market demand for a particular coin. Some truly rare coins experience relatively little demand. Thus, while obviously an important consideration, low population report figures should not be the primary reason for buying a particular coin. It is important to understand price ranges for coins and use that information in conjunction with rarity and other factors to determine if the coin is a good value.

Pitfall #3: Always Take Delivery of Coins and Metals

Any arrangement that is not a tit-for-tat exchange followed by immediate delivery is suspect. This includes companies that offer to store precious metals or coins for their customers. If delivery is not made, the customer only owns them on paper.

Beware of companies that do not ship rare coins or precious metals within a reasonable time — at most two to three weeks — of purchase. Most legitimate companies ship promptly, usually within one to two weeks of payment. Most use United States Postal Service registered mail because it is very reliable and cheaper than FedEx and UPS. While many legitimate companies do use UPS and FedEx, especially for heavy items, beware of any company that does not offer USPS as a delivery option. The reason is that Postal Inspectors, the law enforcement arm of the USPS, are exceptionally vigilant and aggressive when it comes to prosecuting postal fraud. Fraudulent companies prefer to avoid that level of scrutiny.

Always request a shipping date, and it is a good idea to have the company email or call with the tracking number. When your package is received, open it promptly to verify the contents. If there are any problems, contact the company immediately. While all legitimate companies accept returns from unsatisfied customers if done promptly, they tend to consider sales final 10 days to two weeks after the items are received. Because of the volatility of the gold and silver markets, sales of bullion products are always final and generally not subject to return.

Pitfall #4: Credit Cards for Coin Purchases

Avoid using credit cards for coin purchases unless it is strictly for convenience or for small purchases, such as supplies, books and low-value coins. For major purchases, especially bullion, most dealers prefer or require cash, check or bank wire to avoid paying the 2 to 5 percent merchant fee on credit card transactions. While 2 to 5 percent may not be a significant issue on relatively small purchases, it's a problem if used consistently for large purchases. Consider that 3 percent of $150 is only $4.50 while 3 percent of $15,000 is $450 — that's a hefty charge for a money transfer.

Companies that encourage customers to use credit cards have to make up for that 2 to 5 percent elsewhere and usually do so through higher prices. Some sales professionals use the credit card option to push customers into making impulsive buying decisions. The use of high pressure sales tactics is another red flag (see Pitfall #6). Credit cards should never be used if it is the only way one can afford a purchase. The fees and interest charges invariably pile up faster than hard assets will likely appreciate.

Reverse of an 1861 Dahlonega half eagle. *Photo courtesy Doug Winter (www.raregoldcoins.com)*

Pitfall #5: Turnover Guidelines

Trading coins is a time-honored tradition among coin collectors, primarily resulting from a desire to own one coin more than another, or to trade duplicates for something one does not have. It is also appropriate when one desires to change the character of the asset they own: An owner of gold bullion might trade for rarities he's always wanted; a non-collector might inherit numismatic coins but prefer gold or silver bullion, which is easier to understand. One might trade an unwieldy $1000 bag of 90-percent silver for easy to handle one-ounce gold coins, convert a massive accumulation of low-value mint sets into high-end rarities, or sell a low-grade coin to buy a higher grade specimen. All of these strategies can make sense from a collector mentality geared to long-term asset ownership goals.

On the other hand, short-term profit motivation can be especially costly. This occurs when someone buys a coin, and if it does not increase in value quickly enough, he sells, takes his loss and buys another coin he hopes will appreciate faster. It is bad enough for someone to play this game voluntarily and lose. It is worse if a dealer encourages these kinds of trades — called *churning* in the stockbrokerage business — as a means of closing a deal their customer cannot pay for with other funds. In these situations, the dealers make money while the customers lose. Every trade incurs a cost, so there is a financial advantage to minimize the number of trades.

A variation of this pitfall is trying to generate short-term profits by rapidly buying and selling coins. While professional dealers survive by doing this successfully, usually benefitting from netting small spreads on large quantities of coins, it is difficult for the non-professional. I know of one individual in particular who frequently buys and sells, trying to pick winners. He constantly complains about how much money he loses.

Pitfall #6: High Pressure Sales Tactics

High-pressure tactics involve promoting a deal that screams "too good to be true." Most of these fall into the category of making a huge financial gain in a short period of time. Avoid dealers who make such claims. Avoid sellers who push too hard or emphatically — an approach that often indicates there is a hidden flaw in the deal. Avoid sellers who use stock market thinking to close a deal. This applies double to sellers who insist that a purchase be made immediately because the market is so hot, especially with regard to rarities. Rare coin prices don't move that fast.

The best protection against this pitfall is adopting a collector mentality of long-term accumulation.

Pitfall #7: Bullion Masquerading as Numismatic Coins

One method of deception occurs when common bullion coins, both U.S. and foreign, are certified by PCGS or NGC. This gives bullion coins the appearance of being numismatic, even though they are common and sell on the wholesale level near melt value. Some companies sell these coins at premiums of 30 to 40 percent or more above their bullion value. If offered foreign gold, look up the coin involved on the World Gold Coin chart in Chapter 3 to see how much actual gold it contains. If unsure if a coin is numismatic or bullion, do not buy it until you are sure. Premiums higher than 20 percent for strictly bullion coins are excessive.

San Francisco Mint employees in the basement where they worked with gold ingots, circa 1878.

Common date American silver eagles in Mint State or Proof 69 and 70 are a very active part of today's numismatic market. These are favorite coins of multi-level marketers, TV pitchmen and large dealers who sell to mass markets. Because they are modern coins with no long-term track record on prices, their current and potential future value can be exaggerated beyond any semblance of reality. Silver eagles are not particularly rare, as mintage figures show (http://silvereagleguide.com/mintages/), so buying common coins for investment purposes that carry huge numismatic premiums because of being graded 69 or 70 is risky business.

Pitfall # 8: Buying Online from Foreign Dealers

Many legitimate coin dealers sell through eBay. However, eBay has also been an outlet for counterfeit coins mostly produced in China. This should come as no surprise, considering the Chinese have a long history of ignoring trademark and copyright law and producing knockoffs.

Fortunately, PCGS and NGC are working closely with eBay and the FBI to eliminate counterfeiting problems. Both PCGS and NGC have easy-to-use tools on their website, which can show if a slab is counterfeit or genuine. At the risk of sounding xenophobic, do not buy from foreign dealers on eBay or other internet sites unless they are known to be credible.

Pitfall #9: Inadequate Security

See Chapter 11.

Chapter Eleven

Security Concerns and Precautions

UNDOUBTEDLY THE BIGGEST SECURITY PROBLEM with coins and precious metals is theft, as they are small, portable and relatively hard to trace — tempting targets for thieves and other miscreants.

If you are ever the victim of theft, immediately contact the Numismatic Crime Information Center at www.numismaticcrimes. org. This organization has experience working with law enforcement and will help get out the word to rare coin dealers and pawn shops, where thieves might try to sell stolen items.

Insurance

It is a good idea to insure any sizeable coin collection. Like art, rare coins are not covered by regular home insurance. Specialized insurance for coins can usually be purchased from your insurance broker. The American Numismatic Association also lists insurance companies that specialize in coin insurance under "member benefits" on their website (www.money.org).

Insurance for non-dealer collectors can start as low as $50 a year for up to $20,000 in coins stored in a bank vault. Rates are higher if coins are stored at home. Like all insurance, the more coverage and the less secure the storage option, the higher the premium. Collections valued up to $100,000 stored at home or office will typically run in the $250 to $400 range per year. Variables include whether the coins are kept in a safe or not, if the house has an alarm, and how much coverage a person might want while transporting coins between home and bank vault, or to and from coin shows. Each situation is different, and policies are created to fit the circumstances of the individual.

Safe Deposit Boxes

The easiest and perhaps most secure option is to put coins and precious metals in a safe deposit box or lock box facility. In addition to stringent control over who has access to the vault area, specialized keys signatures, and in some cases retina scans are used for identification.

Bank vaults are rated by Underwriters Laboratory based on the minimum time it would take to breach their walls. Class M rating is 15 minutes, Class I is 30 minutes, Class II is 60 minutes and Class III is 120 minutes. Make sure your bank's vault is Class III.

These features make safe deposit boxes exceptionally difficult targets for thieves. Moreover, such thefts are exceedingly rare: I'm almost certain there have been far fewer safe deposit heists in real life than the number of Hollywood movies made about them.

Some people worry that they will not be able to access their safe deposit boxes in the event their bank defaults. This fear is unfounded: The contents of safe deposit boxes belong to the person who rents the box, not the bank. Many banks fail every year, but I have yet to hear of anyone not being able to access their safe deposit box as a result.

There are, however, other access issues. Obviously, one cannot access safe deposit boxes except during normal business hours. Also, in the event of death, safe deposit boxes are sometimes sealed, requiring a court order to open them. Government authorities can seal or seize safe deposit box contents subject to a court order. It is not a bad idea to grant safe deposit box access to a trusted heir who can act in the event you are unable to remove the contents in an emergency.

Home and Office Security

The first and most obvious strategy — and one of the most effective — is to remember that there is security in obscurity. In other words, be discrete. Don't brag about your collection or show it off unnecessarily. Avoid revealing your interest in coins to strangers. If you choose to show coins or precious metals to friends or relatives, don't show everything, and be careful about revealing the value of those coins, or your security arrangements. Keeping low-value collector coins to show children and friends in a separate place from high-value collectibles and gold bullion is a wise strategy.

Safes

Undoubtedly the best choice for home or office storage of valuables is a safe. Not all safes are created equal. Use a highly-rated one that is not only hard to crack, but also fireproof. Extreme heat might melt gold and silver, but it won't change their chemical structure, and they can be reclaimed. The same is not true for rare coins or collectible banknotes. If they are fire damaged, or melted, their collectible value will be sacrificed.

The safe itself should also be secured. Bolt it to the building structure such that the bolts are not readily accessible to bolt cutters. Make sure that tearing through the wall will not leave the safe vulnerable to detachment from the house. I know of one situation in which thieves broke into a house and removed a safe weighing several hundred pounds by dismantling an entire window and hoisting it out using a winch!

On Franklin's Fugio cent, the image plus caption form a *rebus*, which here means *time flies, do your work.*

Frequently, gun safes are used to house coins and precious metals. Many of these are large, expensive, heavy and very difficult to break into. Wall and especially floor safes are more difficult targets than many other kinds. If using a floor safe, make sure it is secured in a block of poured concrete underneath the floor. Both these kinds of safes should be disguised behind a hidden panel or other device. Companies that sell and install safes are good consultants for choosing the best kind of safe for your circumstances.

Sometimes people purchase an inexpensive safe at a building or office supply company. These safes provide adequate protection against casual thieves, but present no significant challenge to someone experienced, even if bolted to the building structure. They can, however, be useful in another way — as decoys.

If a burglar spends his limited time and energy removing a dummy safe, he may overlook the possibility that a wall safe or floor safe exists. Make the dummy safe as heavy as possible. It will tend to convince him there is something of great value inside. Lead weights, bags of pennies and scrap metal are suitable for this purpose. Put some low-value items in the dummy safe that are easy to identify, such as common banknotes which have unique serial numbers. Record the serial numbers, or better yet, digitally photograph the notes. Foreign banknotes with serial numbers are good to include because they cannot easily be spent — but they can be easily identified, which might help catch and convict a thief.

Hiding Coins

Hiding coins is the least effective security arrangement that can be called a security arrangement. It rarely stops even amateur or opportunistic thieves who will empty every drawer, check every book in the bookcase, tear apart the bottoms of chairs, rifle through filing cabinets, empty every box from every closet and cabinet — and that's just to start.

Hiding coins creates another potential problem: People forget where the coins are hidden. Many valuable coins have been lost in this way. If hiding coins, make sure to list the hiding locations and store the list off-premises. The more ingenious the hiding places, the more important the list of locations.

Keep an Inventory

It is also a good idea to keep an up to date inventory of one's coins and precious metals. Digital cameras and cell phones provide an efficient method for photographing the entire collection, making them easier to identify and reclaim in case they are recovered. Insurance companies frequently like to have such pictures on file.

Other Measures

The computer revolution has made available a variety of inexpensive anti-theft and security devices. Most are not difficult to set up. They make visual and sound recordings of activity that can be stored to a file at a remote location. Technology has reached the point where one can use a mobile device to remotely check in on a home or office. These security meansures can potentially reveal a theft in progress. They can also be exceptionally helpful in identifying and finding the thieves. Finding thieves quickly provides the best chance of recovering stolen items.

If the situation warrants, it might be a good idea to install an alarm system. While this flies in the face of the security in obscurity strategy, insurance companies frequently offer a premium discount for alarmed sites. On balance therefore, this is probably a good idea.

Protection from Environmental Damage

More common than damage from fire, is damage from moisture. If living in a dry climate, this is not ordinarily an issue. If the climate is humid, however, put moisture absorber packets with your coins. These are inexpensive, effective and can be used in almost any container. It should be noted that PCGS, NGC and other slabs may retard moisture, but are not moisture proof.

Coin albums, like this Dansco for Kennedy half dollars, is a common method of storing raw specimens.

Another popular way to store raw coins is in collector albums and folders. These can provide some protection against moisture, but only if they are the Dansco or Cornerstone style, where the coin is displayed in a page with inert plastic on both sides. The book cover and cardboard cutouts absorb some moisture. Even so, these are not moisture proof, and coins stored in these books for a long period of time may oxidize. In some cases the resulting toning can be very attractive; sometimes it can be ugly.

There are numerous products now on the market that are suitable to protect one's coins, and they can be purchased from any sizeable coin supply company and from coin stores. If you have questions about safe storage, look through the catalogues of coin supply companies, or visit the coin supplies table that will invariably be present at all but the smallest coin shows. It never hurts to consult a dealer or other collectors who participate in online forums or whom one might meet at coin shows.

Coin security and protection is one area where, to quote Ben Franklin, "An ounce of prevention is worth a pound of cure." A small amount of forethought about security and environmental-protection concerns is liable to spare you from a giant headache later. Franklin also said, "A stitch in time saves nine." Don't procrastinate when it comes to implementing security measures.

Chapter Twelve

Tax Issues

My first and final words on this subject are: Always consult your tax professional to answer any questions regarding potential tax liability related to the buying or selling of rare coins.

The balance of this chapter mentions some of the obvious areas of interest that a tax professional will address with your specific situation in mind.

Privacy

Rare coin dealers are not required by law to file any forms with any federal, state or local agency when customers buy or sell coins, nor are they required to obtain or report the social security numbers of customers.

This situation almost changed as a result of Obamacare, the Affordable Health Care Act. Buried in the original legislation was a requirement that companies that purchased $600 or more from any person or company in any calendar year must file a 1099 form listing the purchase with the federal government. Fortunately, popular outcry was loud and persistent and Congress eliminated this provision — at least for now.

Income Tax

Despite the fact that coin dealers are not required to file a 1099 form when they buy coins, federal law generally requires people to pay taxes on their income and capital gains. Furthermore, depending on whether the individual accumulates coins as a hobby or for investment may impact the deductibility of expenses relating to coin purchases and sales.

Constructed between 1928 and 1936, the IRS Building on Constitution Avenue in Washington, D.C. is headquarters of the government agency that collects over $2.4 trillion each fiscal year from approximately 234 million tax returns. Prior to the enactment of the 16th Amendment of the Constitution on February 13, 1913, it was illegal for the federal government to collect income taxes. *Photo by Joshua Doubek*

Because of this significant gray area, consulting a tax professional is crucial. Legal requirements may differ for individuals, depending on one's income and other tax obligations. In other words, the law does not apply equally to all people in every circumstance. Thus, money lost on rare coin and precious metals transactions might or might not be deductable against income or capital gains. One interesting aspect is that if one buys coins and precious metals but does not sell, there is no income or capital gains to declare because no profit is realized.

Cash Reporting Requirements

There is another aspect of federal law which is not quite taxation. It was designed to ferret out the money laundering by drug dealers and other criminals, and concerns cash transactions of $10,000 or more. It can be one transaction of $10,000, or related transactions totaling $10,000 or more. When such a cash transaction occurs, federal law requires that IRS form 8300 (www.irs.gov/pub/irs-pdf/f8300.pdf) be filed. This applies only to cash — actual greenbacks or currency — but does not apply to checks, bank wires or other transfer instruments of any amount where paper trails exist.

State Taxation

The issue with state taxation usually involves sales tax. All states handle this differently so it is essential to check the rules for the state where the purchase takes place. In most states where sales taxes are collected, the purchase of rare coins or precious metals over a certain amount is not subject to sales tax, whereas those under a certain amount are. In California, that limit is currently $1,500 and applies to the total purchase, not to each individual coin. Limits in other states vary.

The Future

With government at all levels under financial pressure, expect state and federal governments to continue working hard to find a way to tax purchases. Changes in the tax law, both on the state and national levels are likely to occur in the future. It is important to stay abreast of these developments.

One way to do this is to subscribe to publications that report new developments, such as *Coin World*, *Numismatic News*, among others. It is also why I publish the *Rare Coin Report Newsletter* — to keep my clients informed not only about issues relating to specific coins, but also about developments and trends in the rare coin industry and the broader financial markets.

Chapter Thirteen

Getting the Most Out of the Client-Dealer Relationship

PRIOR TO THE CIVIL WAR, PROFESSIONAL coin dealers were virtually non-existent in the United States. Most people collected coins only for face value. There were so few collectors it was commonplace for them to exchange personal correspondence with the various directors of the U.S. Mint, some of whom had a pretty good side business selling especially desirable coins or unused prototypes. After the war, in a time of poor communications and slow travel, many collectors did not have the time to search for the rarities themselves. Dealers filled that role, and a new profession was born. Dealers also provided a quick and convenient means for collectors to sell or trade their coins.

Despite today's vastly increased speed of travel and communications, searching for coins remains a time intensive endeavor. Some collectors go through dozens if not hundreds of display cases at coin shows, or spend long hours looking for coins on the internet. Each collector wants only a narrow slice of the vast quantity and variety of coins available. The extensive time, energy and expertise needed to find a coin of the right type, date, appearance, grade and price remains all too frequently unacknowledged. From the client's standpoint, the question of using a dealer boils down to time versus money.

Services Dealers Provide

The services coin dealers provide break down into roughly four categories: find coins, provide information and expertise, facilitate transactions and buy coins. One gets the most out of coin dealers by obtaining quality services along with competitive buy and sell prices on coins.

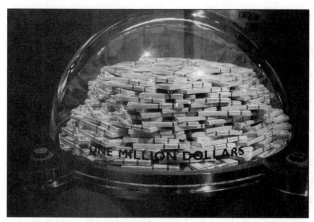

One million dollars is displayed underneath a clear dome consisting of straps of $20 bills at the Chicago Federal Reserve Bank's Money Museum. *Photo courtesy Howard M. Berlin (www.numismatourist.com)*

The goal of most dealers is relatively simple and straight forward: Selling coins for more than what they paid. I mention this obvious point because the best relationships — of any kind — involve trading value for value. Acknowledging what both parties bring to the transactional table is the foundation for successful interactions.

If a collector loves the hunt, the only service dealers provide is having a quantity of coins available for purchase. The customer's goal becomes finding the dealers who regularly carry the kinds of coins he likes. Other customers have dealers do the searching for them. This works well when the customer knows what he wants and is able to communicate the parameters of an acceptable deal effectively.

A collector who does not use the services of a dealer must accomplish the search on his own and for all intents and purposes becomes his own coin dealer. It may seem counterintuitive, but those who hunt on their own may not be able to buy at better prices than dealers can provide to their customers. Dealers have built-in advantages that include extensive networks of customers and other dealers with whom they do regular business. Networks enable dealers to obtain favorable pricing and gain access to coins that may not appear in publications, auctions or online.

As note of caution, it is a good idea to only work with one dealer at a time when searching for a specific coin. One way to sabotage the client-dealer relationship is by requesting a particular coin, and then not buying when the dealer finds it. No one wants to broker deals on behalf of insincere or unreliable buyers.

Working with a dealer to assemble a series or type set often maximizes the value a dealer can provide. Smart dealers work hard to satisfy the goals of such desirable clients, keeping price and quality competitive. The prospect of multiple sales is an incentive for the dealer, making his job easier because looking for multiple coins at once is more efficient. The regular communication necessary facilitates the client tapping into the dealer's storehouse of information and expertise.

One of the questions I am asked frequently from new clients goes is: "I'm interested in investing. What coins do you recommend?" When faced with this question, dealers tend to recommend coins that are in their own best interest to sell. That's human nature, and while the dealer's suggestion may be appropriate, it tends to shift the focus away from the needs and goals of the client to the needs and goals of the dealer. The focus should be on the needs of the client.

The way to make sure this happens is to develop a strategy, and the way to do that is to address the personal questions as outlined in Chapter 1, and then approach dealers. By doing so the client naturally taps into the dealer's knowledge and experience. Enticed by the prospect of new business, most dealers will gladly invest time to help a client develop and refine his strategy and to select coins most suitable for achieving those goals.

Locating the Right Dealer

Locating the right coin dealer is no different than locating the right specialist in any other profession. One of the best ways is through a personal referral. A family member, friend or associate who has experience with gold, silver or rare coins may be able to refer reputable dealers.

Coin shows provide the opportunity to speak with a wide variety of coin dealers, to see the coins they sell, they way they work, and start developing relationships with them. Because of that variety and because it involves personal contact, coin shows are perhaps the best venue available for anyone looking for compatible dealers.

As an important side note, coin shows are also a great place to take children, a fabulous way to spend a Saturday, and certainly far more valuable and productive for a child than watching TV or playing video games. Coins are educational for a wide variety of subjects, including history, economics, politics, aesthetics, philosophy and practical living. Most of the dealers I know enjoy spending time with children as it breaks up the intensity of a busy commerce venue and provides an opportunity to share their enthusiasm about coins.

Hundreds of coins shows are held every year throughout the United States. They range from small to major shows featuring hundreds of dealers. Many of these feature interesting numismatic exhibits.

Major coin shows include:
- The Long Beach Coin Show (Long Beach, CA) held in February, June and September (www.longbeachexpo.com)
- Baltimore Coin Show (Baltimore, MD) held March, June and November (expo.whitman.com)
- The Florida United Numismatists (Orlando, FL) Show held each January and July (www.funtopics.com)
- ANA Money Shows (Each show in a different city) held twice a year in March and August (www.money.org)

Information about shows and dealers can also be found by looking at advertisements in numismatic publications like *Coin World* and *Numismatic News* and searching the websites of the following numismatic organizations:
- The American Numismatic Association (www.money.org): One of the oldest industry organizations, ANA membership is open to everyone at nominal cost, and joining is strongly recommended. The ANA website exhibits a comprehensive list of various numismatic resources.

- The Professional Numismatists Guild: As the most prestigious professional numismatic organization, dealer members undergo a thorough financial and legal background check, must meet certain financial requirements, be recommended by other PNG dealers, and sign the PNG code of ethics and conduct. Dealer profiles are published online. (www.pngdealers.com)

- PCGS (www.pcgs.com) and NGC (www.ngccoin.com): The two major grading companies do a background check, and require dealer recommendations as part of their approval process. They publish a list of their authorized dealers online.

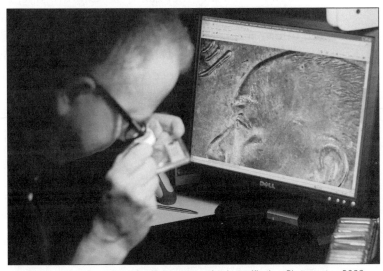

Grading expert examines a rare coin with computer-assisted magnification. *Photo courtesy PCGS*

There are thousands of dealers nationwide, so the field must be narrowed. There is an obvious advantage to using dealers close to home. However, the internet, telephone and fast delivery make this less important that other criteria, including specialty of the dealer, the quality of service the dealer provides, and most important, choosing a dealer with whom you have excellent rapport, communication and compatibility. Finding simpatico dealers with whom one shares these qualities creates a positive environment for addressing a client's needs.

Every contact made, dealer met and customer-dealer relationship developed, whether now or in the future, can lead to acquiring that prized speciman. No one dealer is right for all customers at all times. No single dealer has a monopoly on the coins you want, or a monopoly on the best prices or quality.

While accumulating coins can involve serious sums of money, there is no rule that says it must exclusively be serious business. One of the primary assertions in this book is that one will likely create better financial and collector results by making the process enjoyable. Let's not forgot, coin collecting is terrific fun.

Everyone wants a dealer they can trust. On this issue, I suggest the Reagan philosophy: *Trust, but verify.* To do so requires having the basic tools and information.

It is my hope that reading this book has provided those tools, which will greatly enhance your experience, enjoyment and financial success throughout your numismatic adventures.

See you at the next coin show!